✱ *Global Religions*

Global

AN INTRODUCTION ✳

Religions

EDITED BY MARK JUERGENSMEYER

OXFORD
UNIVERSITY PRESS

2003

OXFORD
UNIVERSITY PRESS

Oxford   New York

Auckland   Bangkok   Buenos Aires   Capetown   Chennai
Dar es Salaam   Delhi   Hong Kong   Istanbul   Karachi   Kolkata
Kuala Lumpur   Madrid   Melbourne   Mexico City   Mumbai   Nairobi
São Paulo   Shanghai   Taipei   Tokyo   Toronto

Copyright © 2003 by Oxford University Press, Inc.

Published by Oxford University Press, Inc.,
198 Madison Avenue, New York, New York 10016

www.oup.com

Oxford is a registered trademark of Oxford University Press

Library of Congress Cataloging-in-Publication Data
Global religions : an introduction / edited by Mark Juergensmeyer.
    p.   cm.
Includes bibliographical references.
ISBN 0-19-515873-3; ISBN 0-19-515874-1 (pbk)
1. Religions   I. Juergensmeyer, Mark.
BL80.3   .G56   2003
291—dc21   2002153780

9   8   7   6   5   4   3   2   1

Printed in the United States of America
on acid-free paper

※

Dedicated to the memory of

Ninian Smart and Wilfred Cantwell Smith,

pioneers in the exploration of

global religion

✳ Contents

Contributors

Said Amir Arjomand is Professor of Sociology at the State University of New York at Stony Brook. He is the author of *The Shadow of God and the Hidden Imam: Religion, Political Organization and Societal Change in Shi'ite Iran from the Beginning to 1890* (1984) and *The Turban for the Crown: The Islamic Revolution in Iran* (1988). He is currently editor of *International Sociology*, the journal of the International Sociological Association.

Harvey Cox is the Victor S. Thomas Professor of Divinity at Harvard University, where he teaches both at the Divinity School and in the Religious Studies Program of the Faculty of Arts and Sciences. His interests focus on the interaction of religion, politics, and culture; Christianity in the Third World (especially Latin America); and new religious movements. In 1965 he published *The Secular City*, which sold over 900,000 copies in eleven languages. Among his other books are *Many Mansions: A Christian's Encounter with Other Faiths* (1988), *Fire From Heaven*, on the significance of the worldwide growth of Pentecostalism (1994), and *Common Prayers: Faith, Family, and a Christian's Journey Through the Jewish Year* (2000).

Harvey E. Goldberg is Professor in the Department of Sociology and Anthropology at the Hebrew University of Jerusalem. He was a Visiting Professor at the University of California, Berkeley, and Boğaziçi University, Istanbul; Visiting Lecturer at the École des Hautes Études en Science Sociale, Paris; and Fellow at the Oxford Centre for Hebrew and Jewish Studies. His books include *Jewish Life in Muslim Libya: Rivals and Relatives* (1990) and *Being Jewish: Cycles of Jewish Life* (2003).

Mark Juergensmeyer is Professor of Sociology and Religious Studies and Director of Global and International Studies at the University of California, Santa Barbara. He has written or edited a dozen books, including *Terror in the Mind of God: The Global Rise of Religious Violence* (revised edition 2003), *Gandhi's Way: A Handbook of Conflict Resolution* (2002), and *The New Cold War: Religious Nationalism Confronts the Secular State* (1993). He has also published *Songs of the Saints of India*, cotranslated with J. S. Hawley (1988).

T. N. Madan is Honorary Professor at the Institute of Economic Growth, University of Delhi, Honorary Fellow of the Royal Anthropological Institute of Great Britain and Ireland, and Docteur Honoris Causa of the University of Paris (Nanterre). He was Visiting Professor of Anthropology and the History of Religion at Harvard University. His books include *Non-renunciation: Themes and Interpretations of Hindu Culture* (1987) and *Modern Myths, Locked Minds: Secularism and Fundamentalism in India* (1997).

Gananath Obeyesekere is Professor of Anthropology, Emeritus, at Princeton University. He is the author of several books, including *Medusa's Hair: An Essay on Personal Symbols and Religious Experience* (1981), *The Work of Culture: Symbolic Transformation in Psychoanalysis and Anthropology* (1990), *The Apotheosis of Captain Cook: European Mythmaking in the Pacific* (1992), and *Imagining Karma: Ethical Transformation in Amerindian, Buddhist and Greek Rebirth* (2002). He resides alternately in New York City and Kandy, Sri Lanka.

Jacob Olupona, who specializes in the history of religions, is Professor of African American and African Studies at the University of California at Davis. He has also taught in Nigeria for several years, where he has conducted field research. Among his books are *Kingship, Religion, and Rituals in a Nigerian Community* (1991), *African Spir-*

ituality: Forms, Meanings, and Expressions (2001), and *Beyond Primitivism: Indigenous Religious Traditions and Modernity* (forthcoming).

Juha Pentikäinen is the founding professor of the Department of Comparative Religion at the University of Helsinki, Finland. He was Visiting Professor of Scandinavian Studies at the University of Minnesota and Visiting Professor of Folklore and Religious Studies at the Universities of California, Indiana, and Texas. He initiated the discipline of Religious Studies at the Institute of Social Science at the University of Tromsö and chaired the Centre for Advanced Study, Norwegian Academy research team on Shamanism. His books include *Oral Repertoire and World View* (1978), *Kalevala Mythology* (1989), *Shamanism and Northern Ecology* (1996), *Shamanism and Culture* (1998), and *Shamanhood Symbolism and Epic* (2000).

Martin Riesebrodt is Associate Professor at the Department of Sociology and the Divinity School, University of Chicago. His books include *Pious Passion: The Emergence of Modern Fundamentalism in the United States and Iran*, translated by Don Reneau (1993), *Die Rückkehr der Religionen: Fundamentalismus und der Kampf der Kulturen* (2000), and *Max Webers Religionssystematik*, coedited with Hans Kippenberg (2001).

Roland Robertson is Professor of Sociology and Director of the Centre for the Study of Globalization, University of Aberdeen, Scotland; Distinguished Service Professor Emeritus of Sociology, University of Pittsburgh; and Honorary Guest Professor of Cultural Studies, Tsinghua University, Beijing. He has held visiting appointments in Hong Kong, Sweden, Japan, Brazil, Turkey, Austria, and Italy. His books include *The Sociological Interpretation of Religion*; *Church-State Relations* (coedited with Thomas Robbins); *Religion and Global Order* (coedited with William R. Garrett); *Meaning and Change*; *International Systems and the Modernization of Societies* (coauthored with J. P. Nettl); and *Globalization: Social Theory and Global Culture*. He has recently coedited, with Kathleen E. White, the six-volume *Globalization: Critical Concepts in Sociology* and is currently editor-in-chief of the forthcoming *Encyclopedia of Globalization*.

Ninian Smart was J. F. Rowny Professor of Religious Studies at the University of California, Santa Barbara. For many years he also held a joint appointment at the University of Lancaster, England, where he founded the Department of Religious Studies. Among his many books are *Dimensions of the Sacred*, *The Religious Experience*, *The World's Religions*, *World Philosophies*, and *The Science of Religion and the Sociology of Knowledge*.

■ *Global Religions*

I ❊ Thinking Globally about Religion

MARK JUERGENSMEYER

Maps can deceive. Several decades ago, cartographers were fond of providing maps that allegedly demarcated the spatial locations of world religions. A great wash of red would stretch from Tibet to Japan, engulfing China, to show where Buddhism was. The Middle East would be tinted green for the terrain of Islam, a yellow India for Hinduism, an orange for African religion, while Christianity's color—often blue, I recall—was brightly emblazoned on Europe and the Western Hemisphere. Some of the more sophisticated maps would make a distinction between the light blue of Protestant Canada and the United States and the dark blue of Catholic Latin America, but there was no question as to clarity of the demarcation. I imagined slipping across the border from a Buddhist red zone to an Islamic green one and suddenly encountering mosques where previously there had been only stupas, temples, and chanting monks.

It has never really been like that, of course. Although there are regions of the world that serve as dense centers of gravity for certain religious traditions, much of the world is less certain as to its religious identity, and always has been. Even Hindu India was a quarter Muslim before Pakistan was created, and even today 15 percent of the Indian population reveres Islam. Indonesia—the largest

Muslim country on the planet—is the home of a rich Hindu culture in Bali and contains at Borabadur one of the world's most important ancient Buddhist sites. China has such diverse religious strata, with most of its population simultaneously accepting Confucian values, Taoist beliefs, and Buddhist worship practices, that most scholars prefer to speak of a multicultural "Chinese religion" rather than any of these three strands by itself. Much the same can be said about the religions of Korea and Japan. In the Western Hemisphere, Haitians are said to be 90 percent Roman Catholic and 90 percent followers of Vodou; needless to say, it is the same 90 percent. Jews, of course, are everywhere, and have been since biblical times.

Today it seems that almost everyone is everywhere. The city of Los Angeles, for instance, is the second-largest Filipino city in the world. It is also the second-largest Iranian city and the second-largest Mexican one. In Southern California, Tibetan Buddhists do not hide in the mountains in monasteries. They drive Lexus SUVs to the studio lot for a photo shoot: some are rich, some are Caucasian, and some are among Hollywood's celebrities. In Beijing the Chinese government has to contend not only with new forms of Chinese religion, such as the Falun-Gong, but also with dissident Chinese Muslims and Christians.

Scarcely any region in the globe today is composed solely of members of a single strand of traditional religion. In an era of globalization the pace of cultural interaction and change has increased by seemingly exponential expansions of degrees. So an accurate coloration of the religious world, even fifty years ago, would have to show dense areas of color here and there, with enormous mixes and shadings of hues everywhere else. Moreover, the map would have to be changed from time to time, perhaps even from decade to decade, and retinted as religions move and intertwine.

This fluid process of cultural interaction, expansion, synthesis, borrowing, and change has been going on from the earliest reaches of recorded history. In fact, the most ancient epic to which we have access—the Gilgamesh Epic of ancient Sumeria some 2,000 years before the time of Christ—tells the story of a great flood brought on by divine wrath, and a human who built an ark to escape it. It is a story retold within the context of the biblical Book of Genesis and now respected by the great religious traditions of Judaism, Christianity, and Islam. The historian of religion Wilfred Cantwell

Smith was fond of pointing out that even as ordinary an artifact as a string of prayer beads illustrates the interaction of religions: Smith speculated that the Roman Catholic idea of the rosary was borrowed from Buddhists in central Asia who in turn stole the idea from Brahmans in Hindu India. The expansion of Christianity from the Mediterranean world into Europe was a gradual one, involving "archipelagos of centrality in a sea of insouciance," as the historian Peter Brown described it. Along the way Christianity picked up many pre-Christian indigenous European cultural practices, including the idea of saints and the festival seasons of Christmas and Easter—the latter named for Eostre, the pagan goddess of spring.

Religion therefore has always been global, in the sense that religious communities and traditions have always maintained permeable boundaries. They have moved, shifted, and interacted with one another around the globe. If one thinks of religion as the cultural expression of a people's sense of ultimate significance, it is understandable that these cultural elements would move as people have moved, and that they would interact and change over time just as people have. Though most religious traditions claim some ultimate anchors of truth that are unchangeable, it is indisputable that every tradition contains within it an enormous diversity of characteristics and myriad cultural elements gleaned from its neighbors.

All this is part of the globalization of religion. Religion is global in that it is related to the global transportation of peoples and the transnational acceptance of religious ideas. There is also a third way that religion is global, which might be called the religion of globalization—in which forms of new religion emerge as expressions of new interactive cultures. In this volume we will consider all three kinds of religious globalization: diasporas, transnational religion, and the religion of plural societies.

✴

Global Diasporas

The term *diaspora* comes from a Greek word meaning "to scatter," and it referred originally to the dispersion of the Jewish people and their culture. The first diaspora was in biblical times, when Israeli kingdoms were conquered and the Jewish people taken into Babylonian captivity. The second occurred after the fall of the Jerusalem Temple in 70 C.E., with Jews scattered around the Mediterranean world—and later dispersed to Europe and much of the rest of the planet. Perhaps no religious tradition has had such a long-sustained existence without a geographic homeland as Judaism. It is the very paradigm of a transnational, diasporic culture.

Judaism is not, however, the only religious tradition whose members have been scattered far and wide, taking their customs and loyalties with them. Increasingly every religious tradition is a religion in diaspora. There are Pakistani Muslims in New Jersey, Tibetan Buddhists in Germany, and European Catholics in Hong Kong. The rapid and easy mobility of people has produced expatriate communities of dispersed cultures around the globe. Almost half of the world's 12 million Sikhs, for instance, live outside their native area of Punjab in northern India. There are large concentrations of Sikhs in Houston, Washington, D.C., and Northern California; others are to be found in London, Africa, and Singapore. Though one thinks of Hinduism as the religion of the people of India, Hindus have traveled abroad and settled in such diverse places as Trinidad and Fiji, where they make up almost half the populations.

In these cases we are talking about people moving from place to place and taking their old religion with them. But when they settle in a locale as an expatriate community, we are talking about the possibilities of new forms of religion, as they interact with the cultures around them. Sometimes this interaction is hostile, as Sikhs discovered when they had to confront the prejudices of European Americans in California in the early part of the twentieth century, or as Hindus have found when they tried to flex their political muscle among the indigenous population of the South Pacific island nation of Fiji. But regardless of hostile responses from local populations, in time a certain amount of cultural interaction occurs whether it is wanted or not.

In the Sikh community in the United States, the older generation has been deeply suspicious of attempts to "Americanize" Sikh culture. Disputes have arisen over such matters as whether young Sikh women should go on dates with non-Sikhs, whether Sikh men should shave their beards, and whether those attending a Sikh function in America should be allowed to sit at a table to eat rather than sitting India-style on the floor. The more conservative members think—correctly—that their culture is changing. At the same time, Sikhs in the Punjab fear that the sheer size of the Sikh community abroad, the diffusion of the religion's authority around the world, and the steady erosion of traditional cultural practices in these expatriate societies are changing the nature of Sikhism as a whole. And they, too, are right.

The global diasporas of peoples and cultures can transform traditions. Though it is likely that Sikhs will retain certain fundamental elements of their tradition—just as Jews and Chinese have in expatriate communities that they have established abroad—it is also likely that there will be changes. They will face some of the issues of acculturation and transformation that Judaism has encountered, some that go to the core of their religion. For example, can outsiders convert to Sikhism? Or is it a religion, as some Jews claim about their own community, that is defined by a distinct ethnic character that can only be demarcated by kinship? The way a community deals with questions such as these will shape the way that Sikhism and other religions in diaspora become global religions.

※

Transnational Religion

In other religious traditions, such as Islam, Christianity, and Buddhism, there is no doubt about whether outsiders can convert to the faith. In these traditions, the very core of their faith includes the notion that their religion is greater than any local group and cannot be confined to the cultural boundaries of any particular region. These are religious traditions with universal pretensions and global ambitions. It is a hallmark of Muslims, Christians, and Buddhists that they believe that their religious ideas are universally applicable. The followers of each of these competitive global ideologies often regard their faith as intellectually superior to the others; some adherents feel that their own traditions alone have a birthright to inherit the earth.

These are transnational religions, religions of expansion. But they also have geographic and cultural roots. Buddhists revere Sarnath, where the Buddha first preached, and study the Sanskrit and Pali of early Buddhist texts. Muslims go on pilgrimage to Mecca, where the message of Allah was revealed to the prophet Muhammad, and respect the Arabic language in which that revelation was made. Christians have a certain appreciation for Jerusalem; Roman Catholic Christians look to Rome and learn the Latin, Hebrew, and Greek of their textual tradition.

Yet despite these emblems of cultural homogeneity, all these traditions are remarkably diverse—held together only by their cores of central ideas, images, and customs. Because these are thought to be universal, they must be available to everyone. And as the many everyones join the faiths and adopt these central teachings and practices to their own contexts, the religions take on a rich diversity. Yet despite the cultural differences between the celebrity Buddhists of Los Angeles and the chanting monks in Chinese villages, constants remain. Although there are many kinds of Buddhists, and thus many Buddhisms—and for that matter, many Christianities and Islams—the interesting feature of transnational religion is its ability to transcend any particular region's claims.

Perhaps for this reason there has been a persistent tension between transnational religions and the state. Political leaders have employed Buddhism, Islam, and Christianity as ideologies of conquest in their attempts to subdue regions over which they have triumphed militarily. When the Spanish conquistadors marched into South America during the seventeenth century, for instance, they were accompanied by priests. The idea was not just to spread the religion and win more souls for Christ; the Spanish also hoped to domesticize the native population and make it more susceptible to rule through what they regarded as the civilizing process of religious conversion. The goals of Buddhist military leaders in central Asia and Muslim generals in the Middle East were much the same.

Yet although religion and politics have been linked through the ages, transnational religions have not been very reliable allies for state power. The same Christianity, Buddhism, and Islam that provide for some rulers a supportive ideology have been for others a basis for rebellion. By latching on to their ideologies, some rulers may think they are harnessing religion's vision of global expansion for their own political fortunes. But it is just as likely that these same religions could be the resource for antinational or transnational forces that would undermine the legitimacy and support of state power. Such is the tension in Islam at the dawn of the twenty-first century between new religious nationalisms in such states as Iran, Afghanistan, and the Sudan, and the transnational guerrilla forces of Islamic activists such as Osama bin Laden's al Qaeda warriors, whose activities and organizations are beyond any national borders. Although these rogue transnational activists find safe harbor in some Muslim states, the contradiction between their purposes sometimes leads them to be at odds.

✳

The Religion of Global Societies

This contradiction between transnational religion and the religion of nations is overcome in instances where religion is itself the expression of a transnational culture and society. The early Christian church is an interesting example. Although Christianity had its roots in Jewish messianism, the apostle Paul brought the transnational elements of Jesus' teachings to the Mediterranean world. This was a region studded with dense population centers much like today's cosmopolitan global cities. In Paul's day, the urban communities of Rome, Antioch, and Corinth comprised multiple ethnic groups—displaced persons uprooted from their traditional cultures and religions, thrown together in urban melting pots. In such simmering contexts, new religions were concocted; many of them thrived. The worship of Roman gods, Gnostic ideas from Greek culture, the deity cults from Egypt, astrological sects from Persia—all of these competed with the radical Jewish group of Christians for the multicultural population's attention and support.

Ultimately Christianity won. It did so for a variety of reasons—one was sheer luck, as the emperor Constantine decided to honor a vision he had during a dream and in 325 C.E. made Christianity the state religion of the Roman Empire. But Christianity had more than Constantine's imprimatur: it had an appeal of its own. Part of this attraction came from the transnational character of its central messages of love, salvation, and redemption. Another part of its appeal was global. Christianity had within a hundred years or so of its existence in the Mediterranean world become a religion of a multicultural population. It had absorbed into its beliefs the idea of the Logos from gnosticism, the devil and the promise of heaven from Zoroastrianism, messianic prophecy from Judaism, and civic responsibility from Roman emperor worship. Its ideas were therefore eclectic, touching many of the traditional beliefs of its potential adherents. Its practices were also portable—relying on prayer and worship that could be performed virtually anywhere. And its ability to create its own community and lines of authority was a powerful appeal to people who came from fragmented backgrounds and felt displaced and alienated from the cultures in which they found themselves.

The people of the Mediterranean world were much like the urban populations of global centers today. But official forms of Christianity today are institutionalized and defensive, and often unable to respond readily to pluralistic cultural settings in the same way that the early Church did in the formative years of the Christian tradition. Much the same can be said of every institutionalized religion. In some cases, however, radical forms of traditional religion—such as the Islamic Ahmaddiya movement and Japan's Soka Gakkai—provide a religious expression for modern cultures. In other cases, it is relatively new branches of old traditions, such as Hindu guru movements and the Mormon Church, that appeal. In yet other cases, this need is filled by new religious movements such as the African syncretic religions and America's Scientology. Still other movements incorporate elements of nature worship and indigenous practices into a kind of religion of global ecology.

Thus religion evolves as the world changes. The various forms of economic, social, technological, and cultural globalization at the dawn of the twenty-first century are the channels for new expressions of religion. New opportunities for the global transmission of religion are created through social mobility and the establishment of diaspora communities, and through the ability to communicate easily the universal ideas of transnational religions to their expanding communities worldwide. As populations merge in plural societies, religions of globalization emerge as well. In an era of shared communication, culture, and ideas, it may be possible to imagine the evolution of a global civilization with its own global religion. Widely revered figures such as Mohandas Gandhi, Desmond Tutu, the Dalai Lama, and Mother Theresa may be the forebears of such a religion's pantheon of saints. As in the past, religion in the future is certain to adapt as it responds to changes in the world around it.

※

Thinking about Religion Globally

This volume is intended to help expand our thinking about the way that religion is evolving in the emerging era of globalization. Most studies of religion focus on single traditions, and even these studies often present the traditions as if they were discrete, immutable entities that seldom change or interact with the cultures around them. Religions' own philosophical and theological understanding, however, has often been more sensitive to the existence of other religions. The writings of the early communities of both Islam and Sikhism contain appreciative comments about the various religious cultures around them and display attempts to appropriate these religions within their own theologies. Christian theologians in recent centuries have become increasingly aware of the necessity of positioning their own understandings of God within a multicultural context. The early nineteenth-century theologian Friedrich Schleiermacher posited true religion as transcending the dogmatic limitations of confessional faith. The nineteenth-century Danish theologian Søren Kierkegaard thought that a natural religiosity lay beneath the apparent diversity of religious traditions. Early in the twentieth century, F. S. C. Northrop wrote about the "meeting of East and West"; William Ernest Hocking imagined an evolved form of Christianity in a transforming interaction with other faiths in what he thought to be the "coming world civilization"; and Arend van Leeuwen understood Christianity's role in world history as one of leading all religions into a global secularism that would transcend the cultural limitations of particular religious creeds. One of the last writings of the twentieth-century Protestant theologian Paul Tillich was devoted to Christianity's encounter with other faiths and the necessity of moving beyond a religious exclusivism. In the twenty first century, the Roman Catholic theologian Hans Kung proposed a global interfaith ethic to be endorsed by all the world's religious communities.

The field of comparative religion that developed in the twentieth century also contributed to the idea that a universal form of religion could link all faiths together. Although most comparative studies limited themselves to the objective analysis of the similarities and differences among religious traditions, some ventured into subjective speculation about the universal elements of religiosity. One of the mid–twentieth century's best-known comparative religionists, Mircea Eliade, who studied the myths and rituals of ancient and arcane cultures, was sometimes accused of advocating the idea of an essential religion to be found at the heart of all mythic imagination. Joseph Campbell, relying on the psychological insights of Carl Jung, made explicit what he thought were religion's common archetypes. Huston Smith mined the ideas of the great religious traditions to discern a "perennial philosophy" found within them all. And the Harvard scholar of comparative religion Wilfred Cantwell Smith proposed that a "world theology" could be fashioned that would eventually surmount the cultural limitations of particularistic faiths.

At the end of the twentieth century and in the first decade of the twenty-first, this somewhat cheery optimism faded, and the role of religion in global society was seen as not necessarily leading to harmony and spiritual union. The eruption of religious violence and strident forms of religious nationalism seemed to counter the unifying trend toward a global religion. The civilizing role that Arnold Toynbee, writing in the first part of the twentieth century, imagined that religion would contribute to world society was in stark contrast to the image of religion in world society portrayed by Samuel Huntington, writing at the end of the twentieth century, when he envisaged religion's role in a clash of civilizations. At the beginning of the twenty-first century in a project analyzing the cultural aspects of globalization, however, Huntington, paired with sociologist Peter Berger, observed that despite the variety of cultural perceptions of globalization, religion and other forms of culture need not always be hostile to globalization and can play a positive role in it. Other sociologists of comparative religion, including Martin Riesebrodt and Roland Robertson, aver that despite the role that religion has played in endorsing parochial movements in the last decades of the twentieth century, it can also be a useful resource in an emerging global civil society. I agree. On the one hand, religion has often been a part of the ideology of antiglobal movements. But on the other hand, the absolutism of religious language and images can help people reach beyond the limitations of their narrow creedal affirmations to a wider sense of tolerance and global understanding.

One of the founders of the modern field of religious studies, Ninian Smart, presented a positive vision of religion's role in an increasingly global world. In an essay on the global future of religion written for this volume and completed shortly before his death, Smart observed that religion was sometimes linked with violence in protests against global modernity. Writing eight months before the September 11 terrorist attacks, Smart prophesied that "weapons of mass destruction" might be used "for religious purposes" to destroy New York or other cities in what Smart said would be considered "the first major crime of the twenty-first century." But Smart also speculated on the emergence of a spiritual and ethical dimension of global civil society—a "global higher order" of civility—that would provide the cultural basis for international order and transnational regulations. This new form of religiosity Smart predicted would be "the coming global civilization."

What will become the global religion—and the religion of globalization—in the twenty-first century? This is one of the questions that lies behind the essays in this volume. Their authors, some of this generation's most thoughtful social analysts of religion, have attempted to understand how religion has been altered by, and in turn is helping to shape, a globalized world. The essays in this volume are part of a larger project in which some sixty scholars have written on the diversity of religious traditions. The larger volume, *A Handbook of Global Religions*, explores the variations of Christianities, Islams, Judaisms, Buddhisms, Hinduisms, and other religions and helps us understand how these traditions are shaped by their changing cultural contexts in various parts of the world. The lead essays that introduce each religious tradition are to be found in this abridged volume.

In this volume we have asked scholars who are close to the religious communities they study to describe how these communities have changed over time, how they have responded to the plural cultural contexts around them, and how they are shaped by the current forces of globalization and social change. The result is a series of essays that not only gives an up-to-date insight into the world's great religions but also provides a broad view of global religion in a new millennium. These essays show that, if the history of religion is a guide, we can expect religion's global future to be much like its global past. The religious imagination in a global era reaches out to encompass a rich diversity of images and ideas that stretch beyond the limitations of particular and parochial affiliations to animate all levels of spiritual sensibility—its social vision and intimate individuality, its arresting particulars and expansive universals, its disturbing depths and soaring heights.

I ✳ Global Religions

2 ✴ *Christianity*

HARVEY COX

S ometime around 1970 the demographic center of Christianity shifted. Since then the majority of the world's 2 billion Christians are no longer to be found in old European and North American precincts of Christendom but in Asia, Africa, and South America. It is startling to realize that the two largest Christian countries in the world, after the United States, are Brazil and Mexico (with Russia and China close behind). Andrew Walls, the founder and director of the University of Edinburgh's Centre for the Study of Christianity in the Non-Western World, contends that both the spiritual and the intellectual center of Christianity have moved to "the southern world." Pressed about what this might mean for the Western church and its theologians, Walls, in an interview published in *Christian Century*, predicted that "it and they will be less significant for the future Christianity" (August 2–9, 2000, p. 795).

Walls is undoubtedly right. Still, I think that it would be premature to claim that the era of "Western" Christianity is over and the age of "global" Christianity is beginning. It would be more accurate to say that we entering an era of global Christianities in which the new ecumenical challenge will be not the relations between and among traditional Catholics and Orthodox and Protestant Christians but the relations among them and the burgeoning new Christian communities that are now rooting themselves in Indic, Chinese, Inca, and African cultures.

This picture becomes even more complicated when one considers that even the Christianity of the Western world is changing. In two or three decades Western Christianity will increasingly have a Pentecostal and charismatic flavor. Not only Euro-American Christians but also the "mainline" churches will find themselves on the margin of global Christendom. How well equipped are Christian leaders and thinkers to address this new globalized situation?

The answer is not very promising. When I interviewed Christian leaders while researching my book on the rapid planetary growth of Pentecostalism, I found that these leaders viewed the rise of Pentecostalism with a mixture of bewilderment, fear, and condescension. They considered the emergent Christian theologies of the non-Western world as picturesque or exotic. The Euro-American theological obsession with "modernity"—a concern that is now nearly two centuries old—has not prepared them to grasp the most urgent theological issue of the day: how Christianity, especially the charismatic variety, can root itself in cultures steeped in Hindu, Buddhist, Confucian, and indigenous religious symbols and still remain Christian.

There are, however, some promising signs. Increasing numbers of younger theologians, from both northern and southern countries, are placing the task of developing a theology of "other religions" high on their agenda. Some of these theologians are Pentecostal.

Among the theological resources for thinking about Christianity in pluralistic cultures is a legacy of reflection that is often overlooked because of the way that Christian theology developed in the twentieth century, especially after Karl Barth. This was a current of Christian thought that took the emergence of world civilization and of globe-encircling religions seriously—something that Barth, despite his towering intellect, never did.

I first became aware of this legacy of global Christian thinking as a child in Sunday school when an overly cerebral young teacher told our fidgeting class about Oswald Spengler's *Decline of the West*. Our bespectacled mentor told us that the whole of Western Christian civilization was doomed to inevitable decline and would be succeeded by a new civilization from the East. In college, this impression was buttressed by a course on world history called "Centers of Civilization," which portrayed religious history in global perspective. In this course we jumped from Athens under Pericles (with Athena and Zeus) to Rome under Augustus (and the fading Roman pantheon) to Baghdad under Haroun al-Raschid (and a vigorous Islam) and then to Rome under Innocent III (at the height of medieval Catholicism), culminating with Washington under Wilson (whose deep-dyed Presbyterianism was passed over with little comment). We read secondary accounts, original sources in translation, and examples of the literature of these periods and looked at slides of temples, cathedrals, and mosques. To some the course might have seemed superficial. But it kindled in me a lifelong love of the intertwined fields of religion and history.

With no formal religious study to guide me, I had to pursue my theological interests as a kind of autodidact but with the help of some classmates who shared my enthusiasms. I was fascinated by writers such as F. S. C. Northrop, whose *Meeting of East and West*, with its intriguing frontispiece of Georgia O'Keeffe's *Two Blue Lines*, offered a more hopeful scenario of East and West than Spengler had. I remember arguing with a Bryn Mawr student (they were all women then) about Toynbee. His *Study of History* had just made *Time* magazine, and we had both heard him lecture. It may be recalled that Toynbee thought only a revival of faith would prevent Western civilization from going down the drain foreseen by Spengler. On the basis of very little knowledge of his multivolume opus, we debated energetically what we took to be his thesis. I thought it was wonderful. The Bryn Mawr student, a serious Presbyterian, said his theology was wooly. (She was probably right.)

In seminary I found the thinking to be much less global in scope. I entered just as the intellectual excitement of the Neoorthodox movement in Protestant theology, initiated by Karl Barth and represented in America by Reinhold Niebuhr, was making its impact. These theologians emphasized biblical categories and Reformation themes, and they did it with captivating flair and imagination. But to me something seemed missing. In doing their work so well, they concentrated on one particular tradition and tended to leave behind the musings of a previous generation of thinkers who had evidenced broader religious concerns. Despite my neoorthodox formation, however, I never gave up my secret vice, and I still have those books on interreligious thinking on my shelf, replete with underlining and marginal comments.

When I began my doctoral work at Harvard in the late 1950s, the Barthian wind was still blowing. But there were other options. My doctoral mentor, James Luther Adams, a Unitarian, nursed an affection for this older, global way of thinking. While I was there, both Christopher Dawson and Gabriel Marcel came to the Yard. I listened attentively to both, but since they were only visiting professors, they quickly passed through. Paul Tillich, with whom I took two advanced seminars, had started out as a philosopher of religion. He was then immersed in the writing of his *Systematic Theology* and somewhat preoccupied with rescuing his students from the influence of Barth. This was before his dramatic turn to an interest in world religions, which happened only after he moved to the University of Chicago and taught with Mircea Eliade. When, after my graduation, I returned to Harvard to teach, I sometimes ate my brown-bag lunch with Wilfred Cantwell Smith, who had come to direct the Center for the Study of World Religions. His book *The Meaning and End of Religion*, though densely written, boldly took on some of the issues neoorthodoxy had swept aside. He once actually had the audacity to offer a seminar on the possibilities of finding a "world faith." I suspect Smith welcomed me to our cheese on rye and coffee lunches even though I was a mere rookie in part because there were not many other people around who appreciated the awesome scope of his projects.

But now we have globalization. Consequently, the somewhat suspect questions that fascinated me in Sunday school, in college, and in graduate school are legitimate again, albeit in a somewhat different key. As an example of the heritage worth retrieving, let me cite a Harvard philosopher (who had already retired before I arrived), William Ernest Hocking. He was the Alford Professor of Natural Religion, Moral Philosophy and Civil Polity until his retirement in 1943. His lifelong preoccupation was the relationship of religions and civilizations. A serious Christian, as he matured in his career, he became increasingly interested in Buddhism and Hinduism but had an especially strong fascination for Islam. As early as 1934 he wrote an essay entitled "Christianity and Intercultural Contacts." In 1938 he delivered the Hibbert Lectures at Cambridge and Oxford. They were published in 1940 as *Living Religions and a World Faith*. In 1956 there appeared his *Coming World Civilization*, which included a chapter entitled "Christianity and the Faith of the Coming World Civilization." But, sadly, even before Hocking died, both philosophy and theology had left his concerns behind. Philosophy became absorbed with semantic analysis; and theology—Christian theology at least—was occupied with more manageable, tradition-specific issues. True, Reinhold Niebuhr did publish a broadly conceived book toward the end of his career, *The Structure of Nations and Empires*. But even his admirers concede that it was one of his weakest efforts. He was more at home with the Hebrew prophets, Augustine, original sin, and Calvin—as were most Christian thinkers of his generation.

But there are some hints that the tide may be turning. Once again there is lively public debate over the idea of civilizations. When Samuel Huntington published his famous essay "The Clash of Civilizations" a few years ago, he was widely criticized for pitting "the West against the rest" in the new post–cold war era. He contended that civilizations would now become the major players and—citing Toynbee—that the core of each civilization was always a religious tradition. His gloomy analysis spoke darkly of "bloody boundaries" and implied the real possibility of an ugly new era of holy wars.

Many of the criticisms of Huntington are quite valid, including the one made by one of my colleagues, Diana Eck, that Huntington's thesis does not take into sufficient consideration the fact that the world religions are now no longer regionally defined as they once were. Muslims and Christians and Buddhists live everywhere on the globe, interspersed with a variety of other peoples, creating a "marbling" effect that raises serious questions about whether they could inspire religious wars against another civilization. A second critique of Huntington is that all the various civilizations of the world are being drawn relentlessly into the maw of market culture and the religion of consumer consumption. Thus a unified, if tawdry, single world civilization is emerging pasted together by McDonald's and Hollywood, in which the classical religions may be reduced to folk artifacts and local color. Even if these critiques are apt, however, Huntington's thesis has raised our sights regarding religions and civilizations. He and his critics have reopened an intellectual Pandora's box—though it was never fully sealed. The older, larger questions are decidedly back on the table. It is no longer quaint to think about Hocking's fascination with "Christianity and the coming world civilization."

As we take up the agenda again, however, we must begin by recognizing that a few things have changed since Hocking, Toynbee, and the others. For example, the world religious traditions themselves are mutating faster than ever. Facilitated by their new proximity and "marbling," the on-the-ground interaction among the adherents of the various spiritual traditions has sped up. It takes place not just at conferences but at kitchen tables, barbeques, and in bars around the world. It has outdistanced the capacity of theologians within those traditions to guide or control it. Still, if somewhat futilely, they try. Ten years ago the Vatican was vexed about Latin American liberation theology. Today Rome loses sleep over Catholic theologians in Sri Lanka and Africa who are trying to rethink Christian theology within the categories of those ancient civilizations. The Sacred Congregation for the Doctrine of the Faith, it would seem, is now more worried about the incursion of karma than about the danger of class struggle.

Little by little the cheek-by-jowl cohabitation among the global faiths has begun to influence Western Christian thought. There was a time when Christian theologians could spin out a complete systematic theology, sometimes in many volumes, with no reference to other religions. Sometimes, when the last chapter (usually on eschatology) was finished, they might devote a kind of appendix to "other religions." Even those who took the dialogue with these alternative faiths seriously wrote as though one could round out a comprehensive Christian theology first, and then, fully equipped, enter it into the larger conversation. The possibility that the very pillars of Christian theology—Christology, revelation, sin and redemption, and the rest—should be rethought in continuing conversation with analogous elements in other faiths had not yet seeped in.

But now the seeping has begun. It is becoming obvious to more and more Christian theologians, mainly younger ones, that it is simply idle to rehearse, for example, the Christian doctrine of creation without reference to a tradition like Buddhism, which flatly denies any such idea. How can one discuss traditional Christian teachings about death and resurrection without taking into account the fact that in America, for instance, an astonishing number of those polled tell interviewers (if not their priests and ministers) that they believe in some form of reincarnation? Or, can one proceed with Christian Christology—a topic that I have taught for the last ten years—without reference to the appreciative portraits of

Jesus Christ now being sketched by Muslims, Jews, Hindus, and Buddhists?

I think not. It is also misleading to treat religion as an entity separate from other aspects of society and politics, as we still sometimes do in the West. Today movements that appear on the surface to be secular nonetheless demonstrate unmistakable religious characteristics. Both nationalism and communism became infamous for their shrines, saints, holy books, hymns, and rites de passage. At the same time, movements that appear to be religious frequently exhibit patently secular purposes. Still, despite these changed parameters and confusing borders, the questions that neoorthodoxy swept under the rug are heaving into view. Here are some of the premises on which they will have to be addressed, as we think globally about Christianity.

First, for blessing or for bane, we *will* have a world civilization. When Hocking and Toynbee and their cohort talked about a world civilization, it was still a surmise or a hope. Today we are there, or nearly so. Some perceive its arrival as a disaster, the ultimate triumph of multinational corporations. Others greet it as the golden dream of the centuries come true at last. Still others see it as a process whose end product is still indistinct but which is subject to midcourse correction. But no one disputes the actuality: the global world civilization is upon us whether we like it or not.

Second, religions will play some role in the coming world civilization. What role is unclear. In some places, the rootedness of indigenous traditions throws up a bulwark against the incursions of globalization at least for a season. At the same time, some historians claim that the religions such as Christianity that are already global have laid the foundation for a worldwide society. Were he alive today, Arnold Toynbee would no doubt contend that no civilization, including presumably a world civilization, can exist for long without a core of symbols, myths, and narratives that preserve and transmit its values and meanings. In other words, no world religion, no world civilization. But others contend that the advent of modern science, mass literacy and instant global communication have rendered religion superfluous. For Christians this argument raises the fascinating question that haunted Dietrich Bonhoeffer toward the end of his life, as he sat in the Gestapo prison, when he suggested that we were entering a "post-religious" age that would require a "non-religious interpretation of the Gospel." The deeper question implied by his comments is whether Christianity is essentially, or only accidentally, a "religion."

Given these elusive factors, it is obvious that answers to all the questions wrapped in the topic of "Christianity and the coming world civilization" are not available. Still, short-range projections are possible. If we are scourged by nuclear war, a worldwide economic collapse, or an ecological disaster—none of which is out of the question—then all bets are off. But given present tendencies, this is what we might well expect of religion(s), including Christianity, and of civilization(s) in the near-term future.

First, the painful divisions within religious traditions will continue. Encounters between traditions open and closed, experiential and doctrinal, hierarchical and congregational, dialogical and dogmatic will deepen. Fundamentalist Christians, Muslims, and Jews will continue to reserve their most scurrilous polemics not for adherents of other faiths but for their fellow religionists whom they view as traitors. (These internal divisions, incidentally, make the kind of clash of civilizations Huntington anticipates even less likely.)

Second, global communication will get faster while human attention spans get shorter, altering both civilization and religion. Technology has always had an effect on civilization. The Romans knit together their sphere of influence, which was nearly "global" for its time, with a then unparalleled system of highways. The British plied the sea lanes. America unified itself, geographically at least, with shining rails and a golden spike. Today we have the Internet. But the burden of the information overload is already taking its toll on our limited capacity to absorb, process, and evaluate the multiple signals. Religion in the past has cultivated the long view and has often encouraged people to slow down on occasion through meditation practices and institutions like the Sabbath. We may already be seeing the beginning of a backlash against speedup and overload. The evidence can be detected in the popularity of meditation techniques and retreat centers. The danger is that religion could become no more than a service sector to the global civilization, no longer shaping its values but merely repairing the spiritual damage it inflicts.

Third, the current direction of global civilization will likely lead to nuclear or ecological calamities unless fundamental changes are introduced. Christianity, along with the other world religions, could play a role in altering the course of this direction. Experts differ on what the first global catastrophe might be—of water, air, climate, or arable soil—but few disagree that, unless present consumption patterns change, it will occur sooner rather than later.

Perpetuating an economy whose logic is infinite expansion on a finite planet enhances the possibility of such a disaster. Moreover, the entrance of China into the world economy could strain the earth's resources even further. The idea of 1 billion new customers consuming petroleum and other hydrocarbons, and then expelling their residues into the atmosphere, is enough to terrify any ecologist. Religions have traditionally taught that restraint and a recognition of limits are virtues to be cultivated, not antiquated habits to be outgrown. But will Christianity, or any religion, be enough to challenge the inner logic of planetary market capitalism? So far the evidence is not entirely encouraging.

The capitalist market system has so far succeeded in making many promises of more wealth for all but has produced instead more division and a wider gulf between haves and have-nots. Christianity has traditionally counseled the rejection of excess riches, especially when they are won at the expense of others. For the most part, however, religions have addressed economic disparity with alms and charity. They have not—with some important exceptions—confronted the structural sources of inequality. It now appears that those exceptions, like Islamic notions of a righteous economy, the medieval Christian doctrine of the just price, the Social Gospel movement, and liberation theology, need to be brought from the past and from theology's edges into the center of reflection on the ethical responsibilities of a global civilization.

Fourth, as Christianity increasingly becomes a global faith, it will engage in the selective retrieval of components of other traditions. This is also true of the other religions. To most people, the major traditions appear less and less like discrete entities, hermetically sealed off from one another. Most people view them as wells from which to draw, or as tool kits from which to choose the elements that give meaning to their lives. This often infuriates the guardians of these traditions who cherish them as indivisible wholes—though one might question whether, in fact, they ever have been.

The best scholarship today questions the idea of "religions" as discrete entities that sail through history like battleships in a fleet, with wide expanses of open sea churning between them, interacting at their edges if at all. Instead, historians suggest that the so-called religions—be they Christianity, Judaism, Islam, or Buddhism—are conceptual constructions projected on a past that in reality was characterized more by interaction than by separateness. Historians such as Daniel Boyarin and Karen King question whether there was something called "Judaism" in the first century c.e., for instance, and something else called "early Christianity" that separated from it and was in conflict with it. They suggest that the actual picture at the time was far more complex. The same could be said for the history of what we now call "Buddhism," which many Hindus see as merely another variant of their heterogeneous tradition.

I am not one of those who believes, as some in Hocking's generation did, that a single world civilization will inevitably result in a single world religion. If anything, we may be headed in a very different direction. As globalization seeks to spread its web to every nook and cranny, it is — unexpectedly, perhaps—evoking resistance from local, indigenous religions some had thought to be moribund. It might amaze Cortez to know that 500 years after his conquest of Mexico ("for gold and for souls," as he put it), the spiritual traditions he thought he had defeated are staging a recovery. How else are we to explain the fusion of Catholic and Mayan images that inspired the Zapatista uprising in Chiapas? What is especially intriguing about this revival is that it occurred not against but within Catholicism. This suggests another question for Christianity in a global age. Might the rebirth of local spiritualities —Native North America, Celtic, indigenous South American, black African —take place within, and even under the sponsorship of, historically mainstream Christianity? Might the same process also occur in other global religious traditions? There is some confirmation that it might.

The fifth point about Christianity in an era of globalization is in regard to the expanding role of women. In Christian churches everywhere women increasingly are exercising leadership. After millennia of marginalization, they are now involved in Christian teaching and research, and in ministerial and priestly functions. There is a parallel development in the other faiths, where women are active in teaching Torah, leading Buddhist retreat centers, and interpreting the Qur'an. The question is still open as to what impact this wholly new kind of liturgical and theological leadership will have.

This inventory could undoubtedly be extended. And it will change as new, unforeseen factors emerge. Who knows what rough and unshaped beasts are slouching toward Bethlehem, Benares, Kyoto, and countless other places to be born? As they do, and as religions go global, I am content that Christian theological reflection will rise to wrestle with this ample agenda of global change.

3 ✻ Islam

SAID AMIR ARJOMAND

Virtually from its inception, Islam has been a global religion. It is the youngest of what Max Weber calls the world religions of salvation. Far more than with Christianity, the old dynamics of the expansion of Islam as a world religion have remained in full vigor, even in the twentieth-first century when Islam now has a billion adherents around the world. In the last quarter of the twentieth century, a new variety of religious movements arose in Islam—as in Christianity and Judaism—that have been called "fundamentalist." Although such movements have been a distinctive aspect of contemporary Islamic society, they by no means comprise all aspects of the contemporary expansion of Islam as a universalist religion of salvation.

According to Max Weber, the world religions of salvation are in principle universalistic: they have a tendency toward missionary expansion and intensive penetration of social life. Weber saw their emergence as the first epochal step in the rationalization of life. Although this process of rationalization can proceed in different directions—related to different concepts of salvation and different solutions to the problem of the meaning of life—it is always universalist. The universalism of the world religions gives them a built-in tendency to overcome many forms of particularism and expand beyond familial, ethnic, and national boundaries.

The missionary expansion of a world religion among nations and across the frontiers of empires can be considered the prototype of the process of globalization. In this old pattern, religion is the motive force of universalization. Contemporary globalization, however, is a much broader process. It is set in motion not by religion but by new cultural and technological forces that are entirely secular. The emergence of fundamentalist movements is often attributed to the impact of globalization on the religious sphere. From this perspective, fundamentalism is to some degree a consequence of globalization. Though this is partly true, other forms of social change besides globalization are also causes of the contemporary resurgence of Islam, including its fundamentalist extremes. The impact of these processes of social change and globalization on Islam has its own dynamics, complicating the old pattern of the universalist expansion of Islam, but by no means obviating it. Indeed, one of the things that makes contemporary Islam theoretically interesting is the intertwining of the dynamics of the old universalism and the new fundamentalism. In what follows I shall analyze these interwoven patterns in contemporary Islam by first examining how some new factors reinforce the old pattern, and then turning to these other, contrary, factors that open deviant paths and new patterns of development.

✳

The Universalist Expansion of Islam

The Islamic era begins with the migration of Muhammad from Mecca to Medina in 622. In was in Medina that Muhammad built a society on the basis of Islam, the new religion he had preached to a small number of Meccan followers as the final revelation in the Abrahamic tradition of monotheism. In the last years of his life, Muhammad conquered Mecca and unified the tribes of Arabia. After his death in 632, his successors, the caliphs, fought the refractory tribes in Arabia and conquered vast territories of the Persian and Roman Empires. The major step in the institutionalization of Islam after Muhammad's death was the establishment of the text of the Qur'an under the third caliph. The canonization of the text of the Qur'an as the Word of God made Islam the religion of the book, even more than the other Abrahamic religions. As the literal Word of God, recited by his Prophet, the Qur'an was a holy scripture par excellence. Its transcendent authority made possible the development of sectarian and mystical variants of Islam that diverged in their interpretation of the faith from the mainstream.

In addition to studying the Qur'an, several schools of pious learning began to collect and transmit the Traditions—reports of the sayings and deeds—of the Prophet. The influence of this pious religious learning on legal practice grew during the first two centuries of Islam. Consequently, the institution that emerged as the main embodiment of Islam by the end of its second century was neither a church, as in Christianity, nor a monastic system, as in Buddhism, but the Islamic law (shari'a). The law became the central institution in Islam, as had been the case with rabbinic Judaism. The Islamic law was in principle based on the Qur'an, the Traditions of the Prophet, and the consensus of the jurists and remained, in Weber's terms, a "jurists' law." The jurists formed schools of law and engaged both in teaching students and in legal consultation. Their compiled opinions acquired the force of law. With the consolidation of Islamic law as the main institutional embodiment of Islam, the scholar-jurists, the ulema, emerged as its guardians and authoritative interpreters.

The contribution of sects and heterodoxies to social transformation in the Islamic civilization has been considerable. Modern historical scholarship of the past hundred years has significantly altered our picture of the expansion of Islam in the seventh century and its penetration into the ancient societies that became parts of a vast Arab empire of conquest. As a result of modern scholarship, we know that Islam, as distinct from Arab domination, was not spread swiftly by the sword but rather gradually and by popular missionary movements, often in defiance of the fiscal interest of the state. During the first three centuries of Islamic history, three important groups of sectarian movements—Kharijism, Murji'ism (which later merged with mainstream Islam), and Shiism—played a very important role in the conversion of the non-Arab subjects of the empire to Islam.

The Arab confederate tribes that ruled a vast empire of conquest were not keen on the conversion of its subject populations. It was only with the Abbasid revolution—Islam's social revolution beyond Arabia in the mid–eighth century—that the universalist potential of Islam as a world religion of salvation was fully released from the superordinate interest of Arab imperial domination. With the Abbasid revolution, a society based on the equality of Arab and non-Arab Muslims came into being. It was in this society and during the first century of Abbasid rule that the institutionalization of Islamic law was achieved. Meanwhile, from the mid–ninth century onward, a movement known as Hanbalism sought to unify sundry traditionalist groups, first against philosophical and theological rationalism and later against Shiism. Among the movements that account for the spread of Islam in the formative period, Hanbalism acted as an important force in the intensive penetration and consolidation of Islam among the urban population. It opposed rationalism in matters of faith and insisted on the unconditional acceptance of the Qur'an and the Prophetic Traditions as its unalterable scriptural fundamentals. Hanbalism can therefore be regarded as the prototype of Islamic fundamentalism. Furthermore, by branding sectarian movements as heretical, the Hanbalites accelerated the process of mutual self-definition between the sects and the mainstream. The mainstream Muslims increasingly came to see themselves as standing against all schism and division and advocating the unity of the Muslim community on the basis of the Tradition (Sunna) of the Prophet, hence the term *Sunnism* as the designation for the mainstream Islam.

In the subsequent centuries, however, the pattern of institutionalization of Islam through Islamic law showed its definite and rather rigid limits. Intensive Islamicization through the law could not facilitate Islam's missionary expansion, nor could it penetrate deeply into society. The mission to convert the population of the frontier and rural areas increasingly fell upon a new mass movement, Sufism (Islamic mysticism). Popular Sufism became the instrument of the spread of Islam both into the geographic periphery of the Muslim world and into the lower ranks of Muslim society, especially in the rural areas. For centuries, popular Sufism offered a distinct variant of Islam that was in many ways the opposite of the scriptural fundamentalism of the Hanbalites. From the fifteenth century onward, popular Shiism adopted many of the practices of the Sufis such as the veneration of the holy imams and their descendants, in place of the Sufi saints, and pilgrimages to the shrines.

Since the beginning of the early modern period, a number of Islamic movements have responded to the challenge of popular religiosity by advocating the revival or renewal (*tajdid*) of Islam by returning to the Book of God and the pristine Islam of the Prophet. These movements can be classified as orthodox reformism, since their aim was the reform and purification of religious beliefs and practices with close attention to the Qur'an and the Prophetic Tradition as the scriptural foundations of Islam. An important movement grew from within the Hanbalite fundamentalist tradition in Arabia to take up this challenge of popular Sufism and Shiism in the eighteenth century. It is known as the Wahhabi movement, after its founder Muhammad b. 'Abd al-Wahhab (d. 1792), who had visited Shiite Iran and come into contact with popular Sufism in Arabia and considered both as disguised polytheism. His followers sacked the Shiite holy shrines in Iraq and destroyed the Sufi orders in Arabia. Wahhabi fundamentalism rejected popular religious practices as polytheistic and aimed at returning to the pure monotheism of early Islam with the cry "Back to the Book and the Tradition of the Prophet!"

Since the nineteenth century, Islam has faced the political and cultural challenge of the West. The Muslim response to this challenge can be simplified into three main types of reaction: secularism, Islamic modernism, and Islamic fundamentalism. Since World War II, this cultural and institutional response to Western domination has been deeply affected by an increasing vitality of Islam that has been firmly rooted in processes of social change. Throughout this time, the evolution of Islam as a universalist religion has continued. This evolution has been quite obvious in conversions to Islam in black Africa and Southeast Asia but much less obvious in the form of intensive penetration of Islam within Muslim societies. The vitality of Islam caused by the social change of the last half century had created major advantages for scriptural fundamentalism over Sufism in popular religion, with the consequence of greater penetration of scriptural Islam into the social lives of the Muslims.

✳

Contemporary Islamic Revival

Three processes of social change have been conducive to a broad revival of religious activity throughout the Muslim world and encouraged the growth of orthodox reformist and scriptural fundamentalism. They are interrelated and overlap chronologically but can be separated for analytical purposes as urbanization; the growth of a religious public sphere with the development of transportation, communication, and the mass media; and the spread of literacy and education (Arjomand 1986). In addition, political change in the twentieth century has had a tremendous impact on Islam.

There is a strong historical connection between congregational religion and urban life in Islam. In its classic pattern, cities with their mosques and centers of religious learning have constituted centers of Islamic orthodoxy, while the tribal and rural areas were a superficially penetrated periphery. Movement from the tribal and rural periphery to the urban centers was associated with increasing religious orthodoxy and a more rigorous adherence to the central tradition of Islam. The late Ernest Gellner (1981:chap. 4) offered a model for this process. The scriptural, legalistic Islam of the ulema did not penetrate into rural areas where the Sufi holy men developed an alternative—a more personal and emotional—popular Islam. The puritanical, legalistic Islam of the cities would penetrate into the rural areas through the rise and fall of tribal dynasties from the periphery in alliance with puritanical ulema, making a "permanent reformation" a distinct feature of Islam. With the permanent concentration of the political life of modern states in the cities and the spread of literacy, the pace of this permanent reformation has been accelerated, and scriptural Islam has become accessible to groups in the rural periphery of Islamic societies without the mediation of Sufi holy men.

This historical relationship between urbanization and the growth of scriptural Islam also holds for the period of rapid urbanization after World War II. In general, social dislocation—migration from villages to towns—is accompanied by increased religious practice and movements of religious revival. During the two decades preceding the Islamic revolution in Iran, the expanding urban centers of that country sustained an increasing vitality in religious activities: visits and donations to shrines and pilgrimages to Mecca greatly increased, while religious associations mushroomed among laymen, and the number of mosques per capita in the rapidly expanding Tehran doubled between 1961 and 1975. A similar association between urban growth and increased religious activities such as spread of Qur'anic schools, religious activities of guilds, and growth of religious associations can be found throughout the Middle East and sub-Saharan Muslim Africa.

Considerable spread of literacy and expansion of higher education have occurred in all Muslim countries at the same time as rapid urbanization and have independently contributed to Islamic revivalist movements. An increase in the publication and circulation of religious books and periodicals, and the growth of Islamic associations in the universities are correlates of this process. The growth of Islamic associations among university students throughout the Muslim world has been striking. It should be noted that university students and graduates in technical fields and the natural sciences predominate in these Islamic university associations. Physicians, pharmacists, engineers, and university students were assumed to be secular types but are now shown to be the backbone of Islamic fundamentalism.

The advent of books, periodicals, and newspapers creates a public sphere in which the literate members of society can participate. The institution of public debates and lectures adds to the vigor of activity in the public spheres; their boundaries are thus extended to include some of the semiliterate. It has long been taken for granted that the enlargement of public spheres is conducive to the rise of sociopolitical movements. However, it is just as possible that it is the arrival of the communications media in conjunction with these spheres that gives rise to religious movements. This has been the case with many Islamic movements since the nineteenth century.

An interesting aspect of the phenomenon of Islamic activism among the intelligentsia is created by the recent expansion of education. With urbanization and migration into metropolitan areas, many young people move from small towns and rural areas into the cities. There they attend universities and become Islamic activists in the newly expanding public sphere. The public sphere centers around universities, which are the scene of a new and highly politicized generation of students attracted to Islamic fundamentalism.

※

Political Islam

The resurgence of Islam sustained by urbanization and the spread of literacy has occurred in the context of the modernization of Muslim states and the incorporation of the masses into political society. The rise of secular, modernizing states, national integration, and political mobilization have politically conditioned this religious revival. Observers who highlight the sharp political edge of the current Islamic revival have referred to it as "political Islam."

The Islamic revolution of 1979 in Iran was the most spectacular reaction to the modernization of the state. The Shiite religious institution had retained its independent authority but lost its influence, as well as its judiciary and educational functions, as a result of the concentration of state power and of the secularization of the judiciary and educational systems in the 1920s and 1930s. Taking advantages of the independence of the Shiite religious institution from the state and using the mass media effectively, Ayatollah Ruhollah Khomeini (d. 1989) was able to harness the religious revival generated by urbanization and the spread of literacy and education to a revolutionary movement that overthrew monarchy and established a theocratic Islamic republic in Iran.

Nowhere is the impact of modern politics on Islam more evident than in the emergence of contemporary Islamic ideologies. For at least a hundred years a variety of entrenched and aspiring Muslim elites have produced what might be called an Islamic modernism. Though their political ideologies have been termed Islamic, Islam has in fact played a subsidiary and sometimes only a decorative role. These ideologies include pan-Islam, Islamic nationalism, justifications of parliamentary democracy in Islamic terms, and Islamic socialism.

Since World War II, however, with the Muslim Brotherhood in Egypt and the Jama'at-i Islami in Pakistan, a distinct type of Islamic political organization and ideology has grown out of scriptural fundamentalism. The primary ideological breakthrough was the work of Abu'l-A'la' Mawdudi (d. 1979) in the Indian subcontinent. The Muslim Brotherhood in Egypt was groping in the same direction but did not achieve anything like Mawdudi's ideological consistency until the l960s. In the following decade, the main features of Islamic political ideologies were adopted by Khomeini's militant followers with a heavy clericalist twist—incidentally, not so much before as during and after the Islamic revolution.

Until the demise of communism in 1989, Islamic political ideologies tended to adopt totalitarian models of society and focus on the constitution of an Islamic state. Where Islamic fundamentalists could participate in the political process, as in Pakistan, their ideology was gradually modified. Where they were excluded from the political process, as in Nasser's Egypt, Islamic fundamentalist ideology became revolutionary. A case in point is Sayyid Qutb (d. 1966), who formulated a Qur'anic justification of revolutionary violence that stands in sharp contrast to the conservative authoritarianism of traditional Islamic political thought. While Qutb's revolutionary version of political Islam continues to have adherents, especially under regimes that do not allow political participation, a pragmatic fundamentalist ideology has grown in the last decade. It encourages participation in competitive politics and shifts its focus from the seizure of the state to the control of civil society. The model for this most recent Islamic political literature is no longer the discredited totalitarian one but the currently fashionable discourse of civil society and, to a lesser extent, the model of the global market.

✳

Islam and Globalization

Continuous improvement and declining cost of transportation since World War II have greatly increased the number of pilgrims to Mecca, and of missionaries from Africa and Asia to the main centers of Islamic learning in the Middle East. It should be noted that this aspect of globalization reinforces Islam's old universalism institutionalized around the Hajj—pilgrimage to Mecca. In fact, improved sea transportation since the seventeenth century had encouraged international contact among Muslims and stimulated transnational movements for orthodox reformism and renewal (*tajdid*).

The postcolonial era has witnessed massive immigration of Muslims into Western Europe and North America, where sizable Muslim communities are formed. Meanwhile, there has been unprecedented global integration of Muslims through the mass media. The media contributed to the success of the Islamic revolution in Iran by enabling the Iranian opposition abroad to orchestrate widespread mass mobilization inside of Iran. Khomeini's aides abroad and his followers in Iran were able to coordinate their nationwide protests by using telephone lines. Khomeini's revolutionary speeches were disseminated by cassettes through the networks of mosques and religious associations. The Persian program of the British Broadcasting Corporation sympathetically reported

Khomeini's activities and proclamations, and these reports were avidly received by millions of households in Iran, to the dismay of the Shah and his political elite.

The international repercussions of the Salman Rushdie case also illustrate the impact of the media on a globally integrated Muslim world. The protests and burning of Rushdie's *Satanic Verses* by indignant Muslims began in Bradford, England. These were broadcast throughout the world and stimulated violent protests in Pakistan, which were in turn broadcast internationally. This media exposure gave Khomeini the opportunity to reassert his claim to revolutionary leadership of the Muslim world in the last year of his life. Only a few months after accepting the cease-fire in the war with Iraq, which had been like "drinking a cup of poison," he had the final satisfaction of issuing, on February 14, 1989, an injunction (*fatwa*) sanctioning the death of Rushdie for apostasy—even though Rushdie was a non-Iranian writer who lived in England.

The effects of globalization on Islam are interpreted variously. Eickelman (1998) sees the combined effect of globalization, the growth of education, and vigorous discussion of Islam in books and public debates as the making of an Islamic reformation. According to Eickelman, the Islamicization of social life has been far-reaching but also dispersed, lacking any focus or single thrust. Barber, by contrast, puts Islam in the front line of the global clash between "Jihad versus McWorld." He sees the effect of globalization concentrated in a sharply focused and vehement "anti-Western anti-universalist struggle" (Barber 1995: 207). Barber obliterates the distinction between Islamic fundamentalism and Islam. It is not just Islamic fundamentalism but Islam, *tout court*, that nurtures conditions favorable to Jihad: "parochialism, anti-modernism, exclusiveness and hostility to 'others'" (205).

I believe Barber's view on Islam and globalization, which is widely shared by journalists and commentators, is fundamentally mistaken. Not only is there variety in Islamic fundamentalism (Arjomand 1995), but Islamic fundamentalism is by no means identical with all the contemporary manifestations of Islam as a universalist religion. Urbanization, development of roads and transportation, the printing revolution, and other contemporary processes of social change, including globalization, all reinforce trends toward expansion and intensive penetration of society that are typical of Islam as a universalist religion. These trends are not exclusively fundamentalist. One would therefore have to agree with Eickelman on the dispersion of the current trends in Islamization, whether or not one concurs with his value judgment that they constitute reformation. One important question remains to be answered, however: How does globalization affect the old forms of Islamic universalism?

An interesting feature of globalization is the unfolding of anti-global sentiments in particularistic, variety-producing movements that seek local legitimacy but nevertheless have a global frame of self-reference. Global integration induces Muslims to emphasize their unique identity within their own frames of reference—cultures that can be at once universal and local. There can be no doubt that global integration has made many Muslims seek to appropriate universalist institutions by what might be called Islamic cloning. We thus hear more and more about "Islamic science," "Islamic human rights," and "the Islamic international system." There are also a variety of organizations modeled after the United Nations and its offshoots, most notably the Organization of the Islamic Conference, which was founded in 1969 and whose last meeting in Tehran in December 1997 was attended by representatives of the fifty-five member countries, including many Muslim heads of state. This phenomenon is a direct result of globalization. To confuse it with fundamentalism is a grave mistake. It is, however, a reactive tendency, and I would call it defensive counter-universalism.

The dynamics of Islam as a universalist religion therefore includes a fundamentalist trend, alongside many others, that has been reinforced by some of the contemporary processes of social change, including globalization. Islam also has acquired a new and sharply political edge under the impact of political modernization. It would be misleading, however, to speak simply of a shift from universalism to fundamentalism. For one thing, missionary traditional Islam continues to flourish and has adopted modern technology to its growth. More important, the main impact of globalization on the Islamic world has not been the growth of fundamentalism but what I call defensive counter-universalism. Fundamentalism can reasonably be characterized as selectively modern and electively traditional; it is therefore assimilative despite its intent. The assimilative character of defensive counter-universalism is more pronounced. It has already resulted in the assimilation of universal organizational forms and, albeit restrictively, of universal ideas such as human rights and rights of women. It is difficult to escape the conclusion that, despite its intent, defensive counter-universalism is inevitably a step toward the modernization of the Islamic tradition.

4 ✴ Judaism

HARVEY E. GOLDBERG

Judaism is perhaps the most global of religious traditions, since for most of its history it has existed in myriad diaspora communities throughout the Middle East, Europe, and eventually the Americas and elsewhere. There are currently some 13 million Jews in the world: the largest number, almost 5 million, are in North America; about 5 million live in Israel, 3 million in Europe, 0.5 million in Latin America, and the remainder in Asia, Australia, Africa, and elsewhere in the Middle East. The global diversity of Jewish residency has therefore created challenges for those who have attempted to study Jewish society as a whole.

✴

The Study of Jewish Societies throughout the World

A broad view of Jewish life throughout the globe was implicit in the new "science of Judaism" formulated early in the nineteenth century, but the systematic and mature application of sociological thought to the historical study of Judaism around the world emerged only slowly. In his programmatic essay of 1818 outlining the nascent science of Judaism (*Wissenschaft des Judentums*), Leopold Zunz (1794–1886) included statistical studies, but the major intellectual thrust that followed immediately thereafter was heavily influenced by an idealist approach to history. It pictured the forward march of Judaism conceived of as a set of religious and philosophical ideas that had an impact on world history as Jews spread throughout the globe. This was prominent in the work of Abraham Geiger (1810–74), who, along with other historians, sought a respectable intellectual place for the Jewish religion as Jews in western and central Europe sought to be accepted into Gentile society in the wake of political emancipation. A modification of this approach appeared in the work of Heinrich Graetz (1817–91), which, taking a more pluralistic view of Jewish experience, presented it as being made up of diverse histories that were all worthy of study. In his view, different periods did not move beyond earlier ones but constituted varying expressions of Judaism envisioned as a set of religious ideas linked to a people. Peoplehood continued to be basic to Judaism after the loss of political independence, although this view did not imply Jewish nationalism such as later emerged in the Zionist movement.

A more explicit diaspora nationalism emerged in the work of Simon Dubnow (1860–1941). Dubnow showed how new centers of Jewish life emerged in different parts of the globe, enjoying independence from the majority polity and culture and replacing those that had declined. Babylonia succeeded the Land of Israel, which in turn was succeeded by Spain and the Rhineland, and the latter two were succeeded by eastern Europe. Following the historical progression of these centers implied close attention to the communal institutions that composed them. Another social perspective was supplied by Salo Baron (1895–1989), whose emphasis on social institutions was an alternative to what he called the lachrymose conception of Jewish history. His multivolume *Social and Religious History of the Jews* is probably the last attempt of a single generalist to provide an overview of Jewish history. His perspective on Jewish social life, however, is not informed by any particular theoretical orientation.

Jewish nationalism in the form of Zionism also gave rise to sociological orientations. These were often linked to practical concerns. Alfred Nossig (1864–1943) was among the founders of the scientific study of Jewish statistics, and he also utilized the perspective of social hygiene to argue that the laws of the Bible and the Talmud were beneficial in terms of personal and public health. His thesis was aimed against anti-Semitic theories of Jewish degeneration. Arthur Ruppin (1876–1943), an economist and sociologist, headed the Palestine Office of the Zionist Organization. In addition to research on current conditions in the Levant, he authored the *Soziologie der Juden* (Sociology of the Jews; Berlin, 1931), a landmark in the historical demography of world Jewry. Martin Buber (1878–1965), known mainly as a philosopher, often formulated his philosophical system in relation to sociological theory. Arriving in Palestine in 1938, he introduced courses that laid the groundwork for the Department of Sociology at the Hebrew University of Jerusalem.

Sociological and anthropological approaches to the Bible first emerged in the nineteenth century. William Robertson Smith (1846–94) showed that biblical religion reflected the social structure of the ancient Israelites. He was one of the tutors of James Frazer (1854–1941), author of the multivolume *Golden Bough* (1890), who also produced the three-volume *Folklore in the Old Testament* (1918). Frazer's oeuvre, in turn, influenced rabbinic scholars such as Louis Ginzberg and Jacob Lauterbach, but their research on legends and rituals did not contain a systematic sociological component. In another direction however, Smith had an impact on Émile Durkheim (1858–1917), who did not focus on Judaism but drew upon biblical and talmudic material in formulating his general principles in the sociology of religion.

Another major figure in the history of sociology, Max Weber (1864–1920), studied ancient Israelite religion and its transformation into rabbinic Judaism. In his *Das Antike Judentum* (1920; Ancient Judaism, 1952), he sought to unravel the relationships between social structural factors and the religious history of the Jews. He sought to understand how, on the one hand, the religious orientations of Judaism led to Christianity, the emergence of Protestantism, and the development of capitalism, which he saw as linked to the "Protestant ethic," while, on the other, Judaism itself did not lead to these developments but to the creation of "pariah capitalism." His comparative sociological approach to Judaism received some attention from scholars of Judaism but much less than his work on Protestantism or on the religions of ancient India and China.

One attempt to apply sociological thought inspired by Weber was in the work of Louis Finkelstein (1895–1991) on the formative stages of rabbinic Jewry, where the differences between the Pharisees (viewed as the forerunners of rabbinic Judaism) and the Sadducees were presented as paralleling the class conflict between plebeian Jews and the aristocracy in Roman Palestine. This thesis was oversimplified, and the effort did not encourage further work in that direction. A later attempt to build on Weber was made by Jacob Katz (1904–98), who adopted the notion of an "ideal type" in describing central European Jewry on the eve of the emancipation is his *Tradition and Crisis* (1961; original Hebrew, 1958). Katz's work may be seen as a turning point in the creation of modern Jewish social history. His focus on the interaction between religious developments and a variety of social-historical factors, including economic, institutional, and political trends, proved to be more illuminating than strictly Marxist approaches to Jewish history.

Another input into the sociological study of Judaism around the world came from anthropology. The linkage between anthropology and biblical research that developed in the nineteenth century was weakened when anthropology became associated with field research in the first part of the twentieth century. By midcentury, there began to coalesce interest in the ethnographic study of contemporary Jews, with special emphasis on those immigrating to Israel from Middle Eastern countries, on memories from eastern European survivors of the Holocaust, and on varieties of religious life emerging in America. Some Jewish historians found anthropological studies, both among Jews and generally, to be useful in relating to documents of earlier periods. An example is the work of S. D. Goitein (1900–85) on the Jews in the Muslim world in the tenth through thirteenth centuries. More recently, Jewish historians have added a cultural emphasis to their work. Examples are the concern with collective memory, pioneered by Yosef Yerushalmi (b. 1932), and the utilization of anthropological insights in research on rituals within family and communal contexts. These studies add a more experiential and intimate dimension to the understanding of earlier periods that supplements the results of institutional approaches.

There has always been some tension between the strong emphasis on textual study in Judaism and the salience of a sociological approach to history. Zunz's founding essay concerned "rabbinic literature," although his vision was to include much more than traditional rabbinic scholarship. The study of ancient Israel could at first rely only on the biblical text, until archaeological finds began to complement that source of data with both material objects and written documents from the ancient Near East. These, however, often leave a glaring gap between the biblical sources and the other materials. It is difficult to sort out the social formations at the base of the biblical texts, while material remains yield hints to social arrangements but rarely are sufficient to provide solid information. Similar gaps characterize periods of the Mishna and the Palestinian and Babylonian Talmuds. Although much is known about these periods from Greek and Roman sources, for example, the way that external data link up with the textual traditions in rabbinic sources is often very unclear.

For the posttalmudic period, correspondence between the centers of study in Iraq (called Babylonia by the Jews) and Jewish communities elsewhere in the Muslim world is a source of important data on everyday life. This took the form of questions from far-flung communities to the centers, and the *responsa* of the latter are a crucial source of social history even though their primary purpose was the clarification of Jewish law. From a somewhat later period in the Islamic world, a mass of material survived in the storehouse of a synagogue known as the Cairo *geniza*. Known to the scholarly world from the 1890s, these documents were first plumbed for the light they shed on traditional subjects such as grammar, philosophy, or the history of rabbinic law. From the 1950s, S. D. Goitein began to utilize them for the writing of socioeconomic history, as recorded in his multivolume *Mediterranean Society* (1967–88).

Earlier, Louis Finkelstein had sought to provide a sociological-like portrait of Jewish life in Europe, at a corresponding period, in his *Jewish Self-Government in the Middle Ages* (1924), but the data available to him were mostly rabbinic writings with a normative perspective. Some noted historians of Judaism, such as Gershom Scholem (1897–1982) in his studies of mysticism, expressed skepticism over the ability of sociology to illuminate religious phenomena. Similarly, there were scholars who were hesitant about the sociological approach of Jacob Katz.

✳

Diversity in Ancient Judaism

The tension between unity and diversity in the society of ancient Israel is manifest in the relationship between centralized monarchy and tribal structure. First emerging in the eleventh century, the monarchy reached its pinnacle of political strength under David, who established Jerusalem as his capital at about 1000 B.C.E. After the reign of his son, Solomon, there was a split into a Northern and a Southern Kingdom. The former, with its capital in Samaria, lasted until 722 B.C.E., when much of its leadership was led into exile to Assyria, while the latter, which came to be called Judea, survived until 586 B.C.E., when it succumbed to Babylonian power and the Jerusalem Temple built by Solomon was destroyed. Much about the social processes paralleling these developments is still to be understood.

Some stress the encroachment of the monarchy and the urban-based aristocracy on the village-based agricultural sector of society. The emphasis of the Pentateuch on protecting widows and orphans and the cry of the prophets for social justice are seen as reflecting growing class tensions. Another view sees rural life and its associated social structures as continuing vigorously until the Babylonian exile. This calls for a fuller understanding of mechanisms of taxation, corvée, and army service, through which kinship units supported the monarchy, while those units still maintained their own resources and institutions.

Another major issue entailing the link between various levels of society is the centralization of worship. It is clear that the Pentateuchal portrait, in which an estate of priests, descended from Moses' brother Aaron, was designated to serve at a single sanctuary, is an idealized rather than historical picture. The emergence and enforcement of the norm that sacrificial worship could take place only in Jerusalem emerged slowly, crystallizing in the seventh century. The history of the priesthood itself is also subject to very differing interpretations. It is similarly an open question as to what other forms of local religious organization might have arisen as the ritual hegemony of Jerusalem became established.

There was a strong linkage between the priesthood and the emerging sacred literature. At the same time, there were other sources of religious inspiration in the form of the literary prophets appearing in the eighth century. The extent to which literacy was widespread in the society is a central question, to which only tentative answers have been given. In any event, there began to develop a canon of sacred writings that had several sources which probably were in the process of being merged with one another before the Babylonian exile. Some sources may have stemmed from literary creations in David's court, others were based in the priestly culture, and yet others reflected the consciousness of exile that affected Judea even as it survived for almost a century and a half longer than its northern brother kingdom. In the period of the Second Temple, made possible by the return of exiles to Judea in the late sixth century after the Persian Empire had displaced the Babylonians, the canonization of what we now call the Bible (the Torah) and its placement at the center of Jewish ideology and identity became even more marked.

The creation of the Torah as a key symbol, and the cultivation of the value that its contents should be known to all Jews, laid the groundwork for possible diversity, as well as a unified religious ulture. Some speculate that the synagogue originated among the Judean exiles in Babylonia even though there is no concrete evidence of synagogue life, in Palestine or in the Diaspora, until several centuries later. Early synagogues were places in which lessons based on selections from the Torah and from the Prophetic writings were read, thereby constituting local centers for the teaching and dramatization of societal norms separate from sacrifice in the Temple. The building of the Second Temple also introduced sectarianism into Jewish life. Local Israelites from the earlier Northern Kingdom who had not gone into exile developed syncretic religious forms based on their own traditions and religious influences imported by exiles from other regions transplanted by the Assyrians into Samaria. They sought to join the returnees from Babylonia in the rebuilding of the Temple but were rebuffed and excluded. They coalesced as a religious group called the Samaritans, with a canon made up of the Five Books of Moses and the Book of Joshua. This "sexateuch" depicted the period before Jerusalem was made the political and religious capital of the united kingdom. Samaritan scrolls of the Torah continued to be written in ancient Hebrew script, while the returnees adopted a new script influenced by their Babylonian contact. That experience also made the Aramaic language an important component of Jewish culture, as reflected in several biblical books and, later, in the Babylonian Talmud.

Further diversity was introduced by the Greek conquest of the whole area in the late fourth century and the Hellenization of the region that continued thereafter. Within Judea, ruling Hellenic culture proved attractive to some members of the upper classes but was simultaneously perceived as a foreign influence by many others. The attempt to forcefully Hellenize Jerusalem and the Temple stimulated the Maccabean revolt in 167 B.C.E., leading to the brief reemergence of Judean autonomy. A century later, Judea was incorporated into the expanding Roman Empire.

Far-reaching political changes and exposure to many cultural cross-currents were the background for further internal religious diversity. Josephus, writing in the first century C.E., described the Sadducees, Pharisees, and Essenes. The first two groups are mentioned in the New Testament, while the latter were probably the sect whose building remains were found near the Dead Sea and whose literature is now known from the scrolls discovered in the region. The Sadducees and Pharisees also appear in rabbinic writings. The former were linked to the priesthood; the latter enjoyed mass support and adopted for themselves stringent ritual rules of priest-like behavior in everyday life at the same time that they claimed the authority to interpret the Torah. Within this milieu, Christianity arose and challenged the authority of the Pharisees and their stress on ritual behavior. It claimed that it was the true continuation of religious truths first revealed in the Torah. It demoted the importance of circumcision and the Torah's dietary laws, practices that became cultural markers delineating the social boundaries of the two religions.

Pharisaic Judaism fed into rabbinic Judaism represented in the authoritative code called the Mishna, compiled in its final form about 200 C.E. In the first century, the Temple was destroyed, and in 133 C.E. a major revolt against the Romans was crushed. The former event brought an end to the concrete symbolic center of Jewish life and did away with the central ruling body, the Sanhedrin. Processes that had begun before the fall of the Temple, where an "aristocracy" of Torah scholarship challenged the aristocracy of the priesthood, were given further emphasis. The synagogue developed forms of prayer worship that were interpreted as replacing, while also symbolically continuing, the sacrificial cult. Representations of Temple worship were also incorporated into domestic life, particularly with reference to food, both on a daily basis and on festivals such as Passover. These strengthened the groundwork enabling the further development of Judaism in diverse and separated locales.

Multicultural Aspects of Diaspora Judaism

In rabbinic Judaism, the Torah and its elaborations became the practical center of Jewish life. The term *torah* came to represent not only the Pentateuch but also the other biblical books and the growing corpus of rabbinic literature. Two parallel sets of Talmudic literature evolved around the Mishna, one in Palestine (receiving final form at about 400 C.E.) and the other in Babylonia (final redaction in the sixth century), which became the demographic center of Jewish life. The Mishnaic code contained many laws not directly found in the Pentateuch, and one major thrust of talmudic discussion was to demonstrate how rabbinic law ultimately depends on the written Torah. This rhetoric concretized the notion that Jewish life, even as it adapts to new conditions, draws its authority from the sacred writings of the past. The rabbis, who were specialists in those writings, thus became a key element in emerging forms of communal organization and leadership, complementing economic and political elites.

With the establishment of Christianity in the Roman Empire (fourth century) and the spread of Islam throughout the Middle East (seventh century), Jewish life was organized under the political and ideological hegemony of these religions. Both made theoretical room for the existence of a Jewish minority (under Islam, Jews were in the same category as Christians), granting Jews internal autonomy in both religious life and many mundane spheres. The Jewish community in Babylonia emerged as the main center of rabbinic authority in the posttalmudic era. Even as Jewish communal life coalesced and strengthened elsewhere, such as in Kairouan (in Tunisia), the talmudic academies in Iraq and their heads—the *geonim*—still maintained some authority as reflected in the *responsa*. Another symbolic statement of Babylonia's centrality and of Judaism's unity was the claim of the political heads there that they were scions to the royal line of David. The office of Head of the Exile depended upon appointment by the caliph, and the extensive links between Jewish communities and the center took place on the background of the far-flung Abbasid Empire.

The waning of that empire coincided with the growing importance and religious autonomy of Jewish centers elsewhere in Cairo, North Africa, Spain, and the Rhineland. The eleventh century was a period in which some of these developments took shape. Rabbinic leaders in these areas formulated the theoretical basis of the authority of local leadership and courts and cultivated instruments such as the ban to enforce their authority. Geographic distance, political borders, the impact of local mores, and the eminence of local authorities combined to create regional religious cultures, in particular the distinction between the Sephardi (Spanish) tradition and the Ashkenazi (emerging in the Rhineland).

The former had absorbed influence from both the Muslim environment and the Christian milieu reintroduced to Spain with the *Reconquista*, while Jews in Europe were exposed only to Christianity. One example of the difference is the creation of a permanent ban on polygamy in Ashkenaz, while the Sephardi tradition found ways of discouraging the marriage of more than one woman but did not totally eliminate the practice. After the final expulsion of Jews and Moors from Spain in 1492, there were many locales in Europe in which the two traditions came in contact with one another, but they often maintained their own traditions and recognized one another as legitimate variants. Outside of Europe, Sephardi rabbinic tradition eventually became dominant in the Jewish communities of the Muslim world.

The diversity of Jewish historical experience and the continual expansion of rabbinic literature gave rise to attempts at codification. One well-known code was that of Maimonides, from twelfth-century Cairo; another was that of Joseph Caro, an exile from Spain who moved to the Ottoman Empire in the sixteenth century. A salient difference between them is that Maimonides included laws relating to the ancient Jewish monarchy and Temple worship, while Caro followed a scheme concerning the laws relevant to Jews at the present time. Sephardi literature, including the codifications, had an impact on Ashkenazi Jewry. Caro's famous work was the basis for the glosses of a Polish sage, Moshe Isserles, and their printed publication in a single book in the sixteenth century has been a major reference point for Jewish law ever since. The same period saw the growth of the Jewish population in eastern Europe, and the challenges of autonomous Jewish life were faced in the framework of the Council of Four Lands, involving both religious and lay leaders, which functioned from the mid-sixteenth to the mid-eighteenth centuries. Some Polish rabbis relating to community issues drew upon the writings of their Spanish predecessors.

Among the former Spanish Jews migrating to other European and Middle Eastern lands were Marranos—people who had outwardly lived as Catholics while keeping part of Jewish tradition secretly—who openly returned to Judaism. In doing so, they accepted normative rabbinic Judaism, but the fact that they had linked themselves to the Jewish community by choice, while being fully familiar with another religious way of life, may have enhanced the feeling of Jewish observance being based on individual volition. In addition, extensive participation in commerce within Europe and around the Mediterranean in the early modern period engendered a sense of choice. From the seventeenth century onward, wealthy Jews with connections to local rulers became familiar with the wider society and culture and experienced a degree of freedom from rabbinic authority. The careers of these "court Jews" had an impact on the expectations of the wider community. One symptom of these trends was the weakening of the power of the communal bans. The evolution of burial societies, ideologically fed by kabbalistic beliefs concerning the individual soul, may reflect the cultivation of internal motivation toward religious observance at a time when age-old communal controls were beginning to weaken.

Ideological change undermining the traditional community appeared in late eighteenth-century Europe in the form of the *haskala* (Jewish enlightenment). Jews were encouraged to be active participants in the surrounding non-Jewish culture. A leader of the movement, Moses Mendelssohn, advocated the abolition of the ritual ban within Jewish communal life. Jews were politically emancipated for the first time in France in 1791 and this political process spread eastward. The result was not a complete disestablishment of organized Jewish life, however, as various forms of state-supported Jewish communal organization were created in some countries. With the gradual weakening of religious observance, however, orthodox groups in central Europe pressed to be released from inclusion in the general Jewish community and to be allowed to organize autonomous communities following their own norms. Their ideology, freed from concrete communal ground, could be applied to other regions wherever Jews were so inclined. For non-orthodox Jews, the new loyalty to the states in which they were incorporated paved the way for new formulations of Judaism in which the choice of individuals played a greater role. This is the background to what became Reform and Conservative Judaism in the United States, where these liberal versions of Judaism developed in a context of strict separation of religion and state.

In eastern Europe, the demographic center of world Jewry during the nineteenth century, emancipation made slow inroads, and most Jews did not develop an identification with emerging nation-states. Influenced by currents in the West, however, many did seek to be free from rabbinic authority and communal control. The struggle against traditional religion yielded forms of explicitly secular Jewish identity. This left the field of religious creativity and organizational initiatives to various trends of orthodoxy. Neither the liberalizing trend nor the growth of orthodoxy had much of an impact on the Jews in Muslim countries, most of whom later migrated to Europe and Israel in the twentieth century. In that century, after religious life was suppressed by the Soviet Union and most of European Jewry was annihilated under Nazi rule, a split emerged in which the new demographic center of Jewry in North America was characterized by Jewish liberalism, while state-supported orthodoxy was established in the new and growing State of Israel.

In the context of contemporary democratic regimes, different versions of Judaism have been able to develop on a voluntary basis, while the context of Israeli life has given orthodox Jews the ability to impose some norms upon Jews who are opposed to them. This is salient in the case of rituals such as marriage and divorce that determine the status of children and in conversion to Judaism, both of which affect inclusion in or exclusion from the Jewish collectivity. At the same time, orthodoxy itself is now sustained by democratic culture and institutions. Orthodox Jews are free to choose to live within orthodox frameworks and to select from a range of options, all falling under the orthodox rubric. All these groups claim that their lives are shaped by the authority of the same basic collection of sacred texts, while significant differences among them are linked to their differential valuation of recent and contemporary rabbinic leaders, each of whom is seen as embodying the true expression of Torah tradition as it should be lived in present times.

5 ❋ *Hinduism*

T. N. MADAN

Although Hinduism is associated with one region of the world
—South Asia—it is a global religion in two senses of the term.
It has provided a religious complement to the diaspora of Hindus
around the world and thus contributed to pluralist cultures in such
disparate places as contemporary Fiji and England. Moreover,
throughout its history Hinduism has embodied the spirit of pluralism. It has been open to a diversity of religious ideas and communities. In that sense it has supplied an early prototype of global religion—the religion of globalized communities.

Because of its diversity, the very definition of Hinduism has
been contested. At its most basic, Hinduism may be defined as the
religion of Hindus—the way they affirm their inner faith and order
their everyday life. India is, of course, where most of the Hindus of
the world live and where they have the status of the dominant religious community. There they constitute 82 percent of India's
nearly 1 billion population. This figure includes the lowest castes,
the "Scheduled Castes" formerly known as Untouchables, many of
whom prefer to be called Dalits ("downtrodden") and who often
deny that they are Hindus. If such exclusion finds general acceptance, the proportion of the Hindus in the total population declines
from four-fifths to two-thirds—approximately 660 million adher-

ents. Throughout the country, Hindus outnumber other religious communities everywhere except in the State of Jammu and Kashmir and the Union Territory of Lakshadweep, which have Muslim majorities.

The only predominantly Hindu country elsewhere in the world is Nepal, where Hinduism is the religion of nearly 90 percent of the 20 million residents. Hindus are the largest religious minority in Sri Lanka (17 percent) and Bangladesh (12 percent), which adds an additional 3 million and 13 million, respectively. Beyond South Asia, a form of Hinduism combined with Buddhism is found among the 4 million residents of the island of Bali in Indonesia, recalling an eastward cultural expansion from India that occurred 2,000 years ago. The wide distribution that makes Hinduism a world religion is relatively recent, beginning with the migrations of indentured laborers in the nineteenth century, under the auspices of British colonialism, which gave countries as far apart as Fiji, Malaysia, South Africa, and Trinidad their Indian (predominantly Hindu) populations. The outflow of migrants has increased considerably in the second half of the twentieth century: they have gone everywhere, but particularly to the United Kingdom, the United States, and West Asia in search of economic opportunities. There are well over a million Indians each in the United Kingdom and Malaysia and about a million in the United States.

✳

The Pluralistic Character of Hinduism

Hinduism as we know it today is fairly recent, but its roots go back to the Vedic religion that prevailed in north India 3,000 years ago. Hinduism evolved over the millennia as the earlier Vedic and Brahmanical traditions spread spatially. It absorbed elements from folk religions (a "universalization" of the local traditions), and it also contributed to them (a "parochialization" of the great literary tradition). Hinduism is also a product of the encounter of Indian with Semitic religious faiths, Islam, and Christianity.

Although for most centuries India had no single name for its religious tradition, the term *Hinduism* was coined and popularized by Christian missionaries, Indologists, and colonial administrators during the late eighteenth and early nineteenth centuries. While some Indian intellectuals initially questioned its use, the term gradually gained acceptance. The projection of a pan-Indian identity, cutting across regional linguistic and cultural boundaries, had an obvious appeal in the context of the emergent nationalism of the late nineteenth century. The internal religious heterogeneity was thus covered over: what was a family of religions came to be seen as one religion.

Max Weber (1864–1920), one of the founders of the sociology of religion, warned against misleading assumptions about Hinduism as a uniform religion. Drawing attention to its internal variations and the concomitant religious tolerance, he concluded that Hinduism was not a religion in the Western sense of term (Weber 1958:23). In common speech as well as scholarly discourses (including sociology), the characteristics of religion are largely derived from the Semitic religions of the West such as church, creed, and founder. Hinduism lacks most of these and other features. Although Weber did not put forward a precise definition of religion, another major contributor to the sociology of religion, Émile Durkheim (1858–1917) emphasized the importance of fundamental beliefs (such as the notion of the sacred as opposed to the profane) and related rites and practices in the constitution of religious faiths and of churchlike organizations in the making of religious communities (Durkheim 1995:44). Hinduism lacks both of these and other features, along with characteristics from other religions, such as the historic memory of a founder (like the Buddha) and the availability of a revealed text (like the Qur'an).

Although the Vedas are indeed regarded as revealed texts by some Hindus, the manner of revelation is not external. It rather consists of the recovery of the perennial wisdom of the sages. Modern Indological scholarship has tended to emphasize belief in the Vedas as scripture and also the authority of the Brahmans as its interpreters as essential features of Hinduism. Sociologists hesitate in concurring, for the great majority of Hindus today have no or only rudimentary ideas about the contents of the Vedas. They do not worship Vedic gods, nor do they perform Vedic rituals. Their gods and goddesses come from the post-Vedic textual tradition of the Puranas and the Epics, their mode of worship is eclectic, and their rituals are primarily domestic. What is more, there is considerable variation from region to region.

The regional congregations (*sampraday*) may have a particular god or goddess at their religious center (as in the case of the worshipers of the Puranic gods Vishnu and Shiva and the goddess Shakti) or a particular ritualistic style (as in the case of devotional Smarta worship or the assertive Tantricism). Sociological studies of religion focus on the regional and local levels, for that is the level of observable sociocultural reality. This does not of course mean that there are no common elements of belief and practice across regional and community boundaries, and that the reality of pan-Indian Hinduism is wholly illusory. For example, if the Brahman priest is completely excluded from the religious ceremonies of a householder, a critical boundary beyond the sociocultural world of Hinduism is crossed. Similarly, the taboo on the consumption of beef has gained wide acceptance among all Hindus since the late nineteenth century. Moreover, the Bhagavad Gita (a late subtext of the epic Mahabharata) has acquired in modern times the status of a central scripture, comparable to the Bible and the Qur'an. It is believed by many Hindus to be the word of God.

The teachings of the Gita are, however, far removed from the Vedas. The Gita adumbrates the notions of moral orientation and obligation through the key Sanskrit term *dharma*, which is found not only in all Indian languages (with minor lexical variations) but also in all Indic religions and is widely used as the Indian equivalent of the word *religion*. Dharma is thought to govern all legitimate worldly ends (*purushartha*), including the pursuit of economic and political goals (*artha*) and aesthetic and sexual enjoyments (*kama*). The relationship of dharma or moral righteousness to the other objectives is hierarchical: it includes in itself the others, even though they may seem opposed to it.

Dharmic guidance to action (karma) is highly context sensitive and varies with place and time and with the age, gender, and essential nature (*svabhava*) of the moral agent. One's essential nature is usually determined by the fact of birth into a particular *varna*, or endogamous hereditary social grouping. There are four such groupings, namely, Brahmans (specialists of scriptural knowledge and priestcraft); Kshatriyas (warriors, kings); Vaishyas (merchants); and Shudras (tillers of the soil, artisans, providers of menial services). The Gita virtually reduces dharma and karma to appropriate varna duties (like *dharma*, *karma* is also found in all Indian languages and the Indic religions). The Gita also attributes the proliferation of castes (*jati*) within each category to cross-*varna* marriages and the dereliction of duties.

Moreover, karmic action has consequences of reward or punishment that the actor must bear. From this premise are derived the notions of transmigration of souls and bodily reincarnation—the cycle of birth, death and rebirth (samsara). Weber (1958) considers the doctrine of karma-samsara "the most consistent theodicy ever produced by history." For the devout Hindu there is no escape from caste, for, as Weber puts it, "the inescapable on-rolling karma causality is in harmony with the eternity of the world, of life, and, above all, the caste order" (121). In other words, Hinduism is the religion of caste—an equation that has found wide support in sociological literature.

✳

Caste, Sect, and the Family

Indologists have long described Hinduism as *varna-ashrama* dharma —the morally grounded way of life appropriate to one's *varna* and one's *ashrama*. The latter is one's stage of life, of which four are recognized in the textual tradition: the preparatory stage of studentship, householdership, retirement, and finally renunciation of all worldly engagements. From the sociological side, the most rigorous attempt to argue a critical relationship between Hinduism and caste is Louis Dumont's *Homo Hierarchicus*. Rejecting the characterization of the caste system in terms of Eurocentric categories such as race, occupation, and class and echoing M. N. Srinivas's (1962) earlier assertion that "ideas regarding pollution and purity are cardinal to Hinduism" (151), Dumont maintains that status positions within the caste system represent more than a simple ranking of strata. Being superior or inferior in a hierarchical pattern of relationships is an expression of the overriding values of ritual purity and pollution. Consequently, status is independent of economic and political power or powerlessness. Srinivas (1959) defined dominance in terms of the convergence of high ritual status, numerical strength, and economic power.

Secular values can at best pretend to be of the same importance as religious values, counters Dumont. The complexity of real-life situations may mask this crucial distinction, he adds, but it holds good at the ideological level. Dumont's critics have accused him of looking at the caste system from the perspective of the highest-ranked Brahmans to the grievous neglect of the view from below.

The latter perspective lends credence to the portrayal of caste as a system of power relations.

Dumont's structuralist analysis leads him to discover antistructure, too, in the domain of religious values in the form of sects that break away from the world of caste and its underlying exclusivist values but often end up becoming new castes. One may even opt for a truly radical alternative, namely, renunciation (*sannyasa*), and obtain total release from caste rules. The renouncers follow their own dharma, however, and often become the founders of new sects.

The renouncers turn their back not only on caste rules but also on family values and obligations. Dumont (1960) has suggested that "the secret of Hinduism may be found in the dialogue between the renouncer and the man-in-the-world" (67). I myself have argued that the preoccupation with caste and renunciation has led to the grievous neglect of the empirical presence and ideological vigor of the householder as the bearer of the values of Hinduism (Madan 1987:17 et passim). Through life-cycle rites, rituals of feeding of ancestors, domestic worship of one's favorite gods and goddesses, propitiation of malignant forces of nature, pilgrimages, and so forth, the householder sustains the way of life that is Hinduism. He affirms the values of domesticity and auspiciousness, plenitude, and moral equipoise, and promotes a rich and sensible philosophy of life in this world.

✳

Modern Hinduism: Revival and Reinterpretation

The renouncer's return to the society in the role of a reformer or innovator is an abiding theme in the history of religions in India. The last quarter of the nineteenth century was witness to the seminal contributions of two unusually gifted renouncers.

Dayananda Sarasvati (1824–83) was distressed by the ascendance of the Hinduism of the later Puranas at the cost of the religion of the Vedas. Ritualism, idolatry, supremacy of the priests, ill-treatment of women, and subjugation of the lower castes were some of the many curses that had invaded Hinduism and Hindu society. Internal decay, Dayananda maintained, was complemented by the external threat posed by the proselytizing religions of Islam and Christianity. India's alternative religious paths—the sectarian secessions that Buddhism, Jainism, and Sikhism offered, before maturing into independent non-Vedic religions—seemed to him worse than the malady of decadent Hinduism. He thought that the only correct course was to excoriate the excrescences and return to the Vedas for inspiration. For this purpose he established the Arya Samaj (association of the Aryas) at Bombay in 1874. Aryas were the people who had produced the Vedas, which he considered the only truly revealed scriptures of humanity, and their religion he called "Arya Dharm."

Dayananda's attitude toward Islam and Christianity was hostile. Breaking with tradition, he advocated readmission of those people into the Arya Dharma—he did not use the word *Hinduism*—who had converted to Islam or Christianity, but he regretted having done so. The Arya Samaj was not so successful in western India as it later became in Punjab, where Christian missionaries had been active. Although the Arya Samaj had no explicit political objectives, resentment against the government's patronage of the church was readily translated into support for the Indian National Congress when this organization was established in 1885.

In the early nineteenth century, many Bengali intellectuals were attracted to some of the theological and ethical ideas of Christianity. Evangelical activities had only begun in Bengal and were not yet seen as threatening there. The most notable of these intellectuals was Rammohan Roy (1772–1833), who founded the Brahmo Sabha at Calcutta in 1828—later renamed the Brahmo Samaj (the society of God)—to promote a new syncretistic religion incorporating late Vedic speculative ideas and the ethical precepts of Jesus. The Brahmo Samaj gathered a considerable following, but its success (unlike that of the Arya Samaj) turned out to be short-lived. Partly in reaction to this development, and partly owing to certain fortuitous circumstances (including the overwhelming impact of a devout Brahman mystic, Ramakrishna, on the urban middle classes), Bengal witnessed, in the closing decades of the century, a movement of religious reform and revival among the Hindus.

The central figure in this movement was Vivekananda (1863–1902), who maintained that Vedanta ("the culmination of Vedic thought") was the "mother" of all religions, each of which was, however, a legitimate way of arriving at the eternal truths. Vivekananda is generally regarded as the prophet of religious pluralism. He was also a modernizer of Hinduism, for he did more than most others to awaken the social conscience of taboo-ridden, caste-minded, inward-looking Hindus. Moreover, he had a dream of Vedantic Hinduism as a world religion. Although Dayananda and Vivekananda were unlike each other in most respects, one of the critical similarities between them was their lack of interest in formal politics. Indeed, the latter considered politics an enemy of the true spiritual quest that he considered the characteristic genius of India.

Modern Hinduism found its most eloquent expression in the politics of Mahatma Gandhi (1869–1948). His Hinduism was grounded not in any profound knowledge of the scriptures—although he did write a commentary on the Bhagavad Gita—but in his deep involvement in politics, which he described as the characteristic mode of moral action in the modern age (yuga dharma). Gandhi did not subscribe to the notion of secular politics divorced from religion or morality. To him these were synonymous.

Unlike the elitist emphasis of Dayananda and Vivekananda on the Vedas and Vedanta, respectively, the twin pillars of Gandhi's Hinduism were, on the one hand, devotion to a personal deity (bhakti) and prayer for divine blessing (*anugraha*) and, on the other, introspection and moral reason. Since the ancient ideas of devotion, prayer, and grace are readily accessible even to unlettered people, this helped Gandhi to communicate with them, as well as with the more intellectually inclined. His appeal to moral reason, which he placed above the authority of the Vedas, recalled the post-Vedic tradition of Brahmanical teaching in which "personal satisfaction" (*atmatushti*) is considered one of the sources of dharma (alongside the Vedas, the Smritis, and the actions of moral exemplars). Gandhi thus bridged the gap between Sanskritic (textual) and popular Hinduism.

Gandhi combined a critical awareness of tradition with a finely tuned sensitivity to the challenges and opportunities of his own time. This was exemplified by his deeply felt moral repugnance for caste discrimination. He attached equal importance to the eradication of the evil practice of untouchability and the ending of colonial subjugation. He also had an intense yearning for interreligious communication and concord. He went beyond Vivekananda's hierarchical pluralism by acknowledging his spiritual indebtedness to Christianity and Islam. He considered the Sermon on the Mount in the New Testament crucial to the evolution of his own moral sensibility and preferred mode of political action (satyagraha, "insistence on truth") based on nonviolence (ahimsa).

Contemporary Trends: Religious Efflorescence and Communalism

In the second half of the twentieth century, following India's independence in 1947, an interesting mixture of apparently contradictory trends has emerged. While the familiar processes of secularization has proceeded apace, and the caste system has become more a political entity than a ritual structure of inter-group relations, the concept of secularism has been redefined to connote a religiously plural society and a nondiscriminatory state that shows equal respect for all religions. The continuing importance of religion in public life has thus been formally recognized.

During this period, Hinduism has evidenced considerable vitality at home and abroad. Alone among the world religions, popular Hinduism has added new divinities to its traditional pantheon. The goddesses Santoshi Ma and Vaishno Devi have gained a prominence they did not enjoy earlier. The shrine dedicated to the latter is now attracting pilgrims from many parts of the country, including Bengal, long known for goddess worship. Worship of the Puranic god Krishna, prevalent virtually all over the country, has curiously received a fillip from the activities of the International Society for Krishna Consciousness (ISKCON), founded by the Indian guru Shrila Prabhupada in the United States in 1967. ISKCON publishes religious literature, builds temples and hospices, and holds religious processions and pilgrimages to holy places associated with the Krishna legend. Similarly, the well-organized activities of Mahesh Yogi to promote transcendental meditation (TM), Vedic sciences, and physical culture (yoga) have attracted worldwide attention. From his communities in India and Oregon, Acharya Rajneesh preached a culture of esoteric knowledge through personal experience that was in some ways a modern echo of the traditional path of spiritual quest through enjoyment (*bhoga*) as opposed to austerity.

These movements peaked in the West in the 1970s and 1980s in the ambience of counterculture movements and were more a commentary on the sociocultural situation of Europe and American than on Hinduism. Moreover, following the deaths of the charismatic gurus Prabhupada and Rajneesh, the cults that grew out of their teachings have weakened. Still, god-persons—both men and women—are a notable component of contemporary Hinduism. One of the most prominent among them is Satya Sai Baba, who has acquired a countrywide following among the urban middle classes through his alleged ability to perform miracles and his role in providing spiritual guidance and material succor to his faithful. He has also successfully persuaded his followers to contribute to educational, health care, and other social goals.

Among other manifestations of the contemporary vigor of Hinduism is the salience of pilgrimage as religious activity. Pilgrimage to holy places such as the meeting places of rivers, or other places associated with events in the two epics, Mahabharata and Ramayana, or with Puranic legends are part of the Hindu religious tradition. They have provided collective religious experience somewhat removed from domestic and caste-governed settings. A gradual shrinkage of regular religious performances at home or in temples has occurred as a result of the pressures of urban life. At the same time, the middle classes have been expanding in size, and salaried people among them receive employment benefits that include partly paid holidays (travel by train in India and Nepal for the employee and his or her dependents is covered). A very large number of people combine religious devotion with sightseeing and choose a holy place as their destination.

In recent times expressions of religiosity have been utilized by right-wing political organizations, notably the Vishwa Hindu Parishad (VHP) and the Bharatiya Janata Party (BJP), to mobilize support for their own agendas. These have included, first, a general call for the promotion of Hindu culture as the national culture of India, equating Hindu identity (*hindutva*) with national identity, and, second, the demolition of several Muslim mosques of north India. These places of worship are either known or believed to have been constructed at sites where Hindu temples had been pulled down earlier in celebration of Muslim supremacy.

One of them in the city of Ayodhya, at a place known among religious-minded Hindus as the "birthplace" of the god Rama, was actually demolished by frenzied Hindu mobs in December 1992, allegedly under the guidance of VHP and BJP. The destruction of the mosque was followed by widespread killings of Muslims by Hindus and, later, by a Muslim reaction that took the form of bombing of public buildings in Bombay. These were the worst incidents of communal violence in India after the riots that accompanied the partition of the subcontinent in 1947. The Indian Parliament enacted legislation in 1993 requiring the union and state governments to protect the status of all religious buildings. The question of whether the destroyed mosque in Ayodhya is to be rebuilt at its original site, or a Rama temple is to be erected there, was passed on to the judiciary for decision. What the VHP and BJP has achieved is a transformation of the personality of Rama, emphasizing his role as a warrior at the cost of the more traditional beatific image of amoral exemplar.

The regrettable chain of events that resulted in the vandalism at Ayodhya underscores the communal politics into which Hinduism has been dragged in the present century. Hinduism in the twenty-first century is not only the religious faith of millions but also a political ideology shaped for the capture of power. The spirit of tolerance of Hinduism that sociologists such as Weber and Srinivas have written about, and modern-day Hindus such as Vivekananda and Gandhi have extolled, faces its severest test. Nevertheless, Hinduism as global religious faith is not about to disappear "from the home and the world of most of India's Hindus" (Fuller 1992:261).

6 ✳ *Buddhism*

GANANATH OBEYESEKERE

Buddhism, like other religions of salvation, has had two forms of global outreach. First, through its long history in South, Southeast, East, and central Asia, Buddhism has incorporated village and perhaps even local tribal communities into its fold. In this sense it is very much in the spirit of other salvation religions with a universalistic vision, such as Christianity. This process was aided when kings became Buddhists, following the example of the model king Asoka who, at least in the self-conceptions of Buddhists, initiated a Buddhist state in India. Wherever Buddhism was established, either with royal patronage or without it, Buddhism was visibly present through its monks, monasteries, temples, and symbols of the Buddha presence, such as the *bodhi* tree, stupas where relics were enshrined, and pilgrimage centers where Buddhists from different parts of the larger state or nation could congregate and give expression to a greater translocal sense of communal consciousness.

When Buddhist kingdoms were established in South and Southeast Asia in particular, the idea of the community, *sāsana,* took on a purely local meaning as the religion of the "nation," as it were. *Sāsana* can be glossed as the "dispensation of the Buddha" or the "Buddhist church" in the Durkheimian sense as the community of the faithful and the beliefs and symbols associated with an imagined sense of communal unity. Ordinary Buddhists continue to use the term *sāsana* alongside the other term *Buddhāgama,* or "Buddhism," as I will also do in this chapter. The term *Buddhism* is a Western neologism that has come to stay and, like the sister term *Hinduism,* has become indigenized such that people will say today they belong to the *Buddhāgama* or the "religion of the Buddha" (*āgama,* which literally means "tradition" but has become a modern rendering of the European term "religion"). Though it is impossible in contemporary discourse to do away with "Buddhism" (and "religion"), it is important to remember that the traditional rendering of that idea was *Buddhasāsana.*

In addition to "nation," another meaning of *sāsana* is in the true spirit of the founder and is the second form of Buddhism's translocal, indeed global, outreach. This meaning of *sāsana* is the large Buddhist order that knows no ethnic or national bounds and represents the "universal Buddhist church," if one may use that phrase. For ordinary Buddhists, the *sāsana* simply meant the Buddhism of their nation; but even ordinary Buddhists knew that Buddhism's home was in India, and most Buddhist elites in both Mahayana and Theravada were aware of the larger meanings of *sāsana* that transcended the physical bounds of one's nation or speech community. Throughout Buddhist history, pilgrim monks traveled to parts of the then-known Buddhist world. This double meaning of *sāsana* is true to the idea of a "church" in other universal religions also. One cannot understand globalization in relation to Buddhism without bearing in mind the interplay of the two meanings of *sāsana* and that both meanings, in their differing ways, have a translocal significance.

However much one might disagree with Karl Jaspers regarding the term *axial* and his idea of periodization of Axial Age religions, he was right in seeing religions such as Buddhism, Islam, and Christianity as having a transcendental and universalizing vision, which then informed their missionary activity. Though they were universal religions, they were not "world religions" in any obvious sense. Buddhism did not penetrate fully even the then-known world of Asia; and neither did Islam. It was with the discovery of the New World and European imperialism that one universal religion, Christianity, began to take root in virtually every part of the world, and in this sense it became the first "world religion," and perhaps remains the only one. Islam expanded with trade, but it also constituted a colonial penetration to some degree, though it was not associated with the implantation of religion in the new worlds opened up by the European voyages of discovery and imperial expansion. But the expansion of Christianity came up with an inescapable dark side; it was inextricably tainted with colonialism and the appalling cruelties associated with imperial conquest, something it has not been able to shed to this very day. I am suggesting that globalization provides a means for Buddhism, if not Islam, to penetrate our world in somewhat limited ways but without the shadow of colonialism. But insofar as globalization is the contemporary manifestation of capitalism's world expansion, one must see the beginnings of Buddhist penetration into Europe and America (but certainly not the world) in historical terms.

✳

Buddhism and the European Enlightenment

Buddhism was known to Europe superficially for a long time, but it was in the eighteenth and nineteenth centuries that its impact was felt on the popular level as European romanticism's Other (in a favorable sense) and, less favorably, as the philosopher's Other (notably Hegel's). What influenced Europe powerfully was the book *The World As Will and Representation* by Arthur Schopenhauer (1788–1860), who used Buddhism and Vedanta as a foil to what he believed was the soteriological bankruptcy of both the Judeo-Christian tradition and Enlightenment notions of rationality. Schopenhauer was interested in Vedanta and Buddhism equally, though his appropriation of Buddhism was perhaps closer to the spirit of Buddhism than his Vedanta. Halbfass (1990) puts it well in saying that Schopenhauer "showed an unprecedented readiness to integrate Indian ideas into his own, European thinking and self-understanding, and utilize them for the illustration, articulation and clarification of his own teachings and problems" (120). Halbfass goes on to say that Schopenhauer used these concepts to mount "a radical critique of some of the most fundamental propositions of the Judaeo-Christian tradition, such as the notions of a personal God and the uniqueness of the human individual and the meaning of history" while retaining "the modern Western belief in the powers of the intellect, rationality, planning and progress" (120). At times Schopenhauer referred to his few followers as "we Buddhists" (Kantowsky 1995:103).

It is hard to imagine how Europe could do otherwise than appropriate Buddhism into its own scheme of things, however different such "schemes" might well be. The major scholarly translations of Buddhist texts and pioneer Buddhist scholars whose work influenced twentieth-century notions of Buddhism appeared after Schopenhauer in the later nineteenth century: they were figures such as Herman Oldenburg, Max Muller, Sylvain Levi, La Vallee Poussin, Rhys Davids, E. J. Thomas, and more recent scholars such as Etienne Lamotte. Though the early research was focused on both Mahayana and Theravada, the latter received a boost from the founding and publication of the Pali Text Society by Rhys Davids in 1881, which soon furnished reasonable translations of virtually all Buddhist texts of the Theravada canon.

There may, however, have been a hidden agenda among nineteenth-century Europeans engaged in Buddhist studies. Because the work of these great European Buddhist scholars took place in the wake of Darwinism and the death of God, Buddhism stood out as a religion that did not need a God and a doctrine of creation that went counter to the scientific rationality of that century. Buddhism became a religion without a God, a kind of "non-theistic religion," as von Glasenapp (1970) put it, and in this sense it was consonant with Europe's own Enlightenment. Much of this was true; but it did place the well-known Buddhist ideas of the miraculous birth of the Buddha, the signs of the great man that he displayed, his discourses on heaven and hell, and virtually all of the Buddhist mythos as alien to its true spirit. Thus, one of the most fascinating of Buddhist texts, the *Janavasabha Sutta*, which deals with the Buddha's shamanic-like powers, were ignored or pejoratively labeled, as Rhys Davids did, as an interesting "fairy tale." So were the great popular traditions of the Buddha's past births, or *jātakas*. Most significantly the Buddha's own powerful experience under the *bodhi* tree was rendered as the "Enlightenment," rather than an "Awakening." In doing so this neglects awakenings that were both physical (after suffering a symbolic death owing to the ascetic starvation practices he performed) and spiritual (when he becomes the "fully Awakened One" after the discovery of Buddhist truths through his state of deep meditative trance). I believe that the conscious or unconscious choice of the term *Enlightenment* helped promote Buddhism's consonance with Europe's own Enlightenment and hastened the process where the *sāsana* became Buddh-*ism*, a systematic, unmetaphysical, and rational religion opposed to the unscientific burden (and even perhaps the colonialist cross) that Christianity had to bear.

For Theravada scholars the great traditions of Mahayana were tissues of irrational magical accretions comparable to the very few in the Theravada tradition already listed by us. Theravada Buddhism as formulated by Indologists then had an appeal to a European audience—though as a foil to Christianity. The circle that Buddhism influenced was still a very restricted one, at least in the late nineteenth and early twentieth centuries. The change came with the embrace of both Theravada and Mahayana (as well as forms of Hinduism) by one of the most popular intellectual movements of the late nineteenth century, Theosophy.

※

Theosophy: Rational Buddhism and Magical Mahayana

The impact of Theosophy on the traditional worlds of Buddhism and Hinduism is only beginning to be understood, though the history of the Theosophical Society is well known. The society was formed in 1875 in New York, cofounded by H. P. Blavatsky, Colonel Henry Steel Olcott, and William Q. Judge (Prothero 1996). It was the heir to European and American Spiritualism even though formally opposed to it. Theosophy claimed to be "scientific," and it is no surprise that many scientists (one of the most eminent being Thomas Edison) were members. Early Theosophy believed in the powers of forces known as "elementals." To this idea was soon added a more important one, that of mahatmas or masters (or adepts) who lived in the Himalayas but could manifest themselves in their apparitional forms to specially gifted Theosophists, Olcott included. Olcott had one mahatma known as Koot Hoomi, or KH, who appeared before him during crises and helped him resolve them, very much like spirit helpers in other religions. Though Olcott became a Buddhist rationalist later on, and was critical of Blavatsky's occult powers, he never gave up his belief in mahatmas.

From our point of view the crucial event for Theosophists was the debates between Christians and Buddhists between 1865 and 1873 in Sri Lanka, which Olcott and Blavatsky heard about. They decided to join forces with Buddhists and arrived in Sri Lanka on May

17, 1880, to a spectacular welcome and formally adopted the Buddhist faith with the public recital of the Five Precepts. Elsewhere I have described at length the later development of the Theosophical Society, and I shall here summarize the key events (Obeyesekere 1991:219–39; 1995:32–71). Though the two Theosophists decided to establish the society's headquarters in Adyar (Madras), Olcott paid several visits to Sri Lanka, taking upon himself the task of resuscitating Buddhism in that nation. He founded the Buddhist Theosophical Society, and soon it established a network of schools, totaling 103 in 1898, modeled on the missionary ones, some equal to the best of them.

Olcott railed against the fact that Buddhism had taken over Hindu practices, undermining Buddhism's rationality. With the aid of learned Buddhist monks he soon formulated *The Buddhist Catechism* (1881), a distillation of the essence of his rationalist doctrine and a vehicle for educating "our children" about the true Buddhism uncontaminated by "superstition." Initially, Olcott wanted to introduce Vedantic ideas of *ātman* and Theosophist ideas of mahatmas into Buddhism, but the monks would have none of it. The *Catechism* was translated into twenty languages and went into forty editions in his own lifetime. It seems, then, that Olcott himself, in his relationship with learned monks and through his voluminous reading of Buddhist texts, came to *learn* Theravada Buddhism but from a Euro-rational viewpoint. Olcott's catechistic dictum that Buddhism was a philosophy and not a creed has been adopted virtually as axiomatic by Buddhist intellectuals. Spurred by Olcott's example, a group of prominent Buddhists developed the Buddhist flag, which soon became a visible symbol of pan-Buddhist unity and ecumenicalism everywhere. Few are aware of the recency of its origin.

While Olcott was becoming more and more Buddhist, his colleague and friend Blavatsky was become more committed to her own brand of occultism, which one could label as magical Vajrayana. Blavatsky's occult powers were well known through the popular English press in India. These powers were impressive: she was said to have materialized objects, produced telepathic messages (much like faxes), created illusory palaces, and produced flowers seemingly from nowhere. Some of her writings, she claimed, were not products of her direct authorship but that of mahatmas. By contrast, Olcott, in spite of mahatmas and spirit healing, was a product of the Enlightenment, continuing the Enlightenment's self-imaginings of rationality, unable to see what Peter Gay (1968) calls its "rationalistic myopia" (83). Blavatsky was not; hers was a more eclectic vision compounded of both eastern and western mysticism and hermetic thought. She was a prophetess full of crazy and brilliant insights but by no means given to experimental validation or conceptual systematization, though she did believe that her powers were rooted in a deeper science ("wisdom religion," "transcendental philosophy") that had yet to await its realization. If Olcott popularized a Euro-rational view of Buddhism, Blavatsky's influence was quite different. Its effect was more on the Hindu consciousness, creating a space for a certain class of modern gurus and saviors to emerge into prominence, especially those who learned to validate their charisma by materializing objects. The precedent for these public displays of occult powers is Blavatsky's because, as Olcott contemptuously pointed out, such forms of occultism were contrary to the spirit of both Vedanta and Buddhism. When Olcott and Blavatsky met Vedantic gurus and asked them to display their knowledge of "phenomena," they were told that such displays were the popular arts of the marketplace and had no relevance for salvation.

The contributions of Olcott and Blavatsky can be viewed from another perspective. Whether or not they directly influenced the many Buddhisms of the West, they exemplified two important strands in exported Buddhism: one that found Buddhism consonant with the European Enlightenment and the other that stood diametrically opposed to it. Regarding the former, Martin Baumann (1995) says insightfully of Europeans, prior to the 1960s: "Buddhism [in Germany and Europe in general] was praised as a scientific and analytical religion which did not contradict the findings of modern science." Rather, Baumann claimed, "it confirmed the results of modern biology or physics and thus amounted to the religion of the modern age" (82). Parallel with this orientation is a selective return to the Pali canon to restore the original teachings of the Buddha without resort to cosmology and metaphysics. For much of Europe this purified Buddhism, according to Baumann, could be seen as a form of "Protestant Buddhism," a term that I invented to designate the absorption by Buddhists in the late nineteenth century of colonial and Protestant values. By contrast, Blavatsky's teachings were fundamentally concerned with cosmology and metaphysics. As a founding figure of the later counterculture and New Age religions, she produced work that expectably extolled the enchanted world of magic, astrology, popular notions of karma and rebirth, and mysticism (defined as the production of "phenomena"; Hanegraaff, 1996).

✳

Globalization, Diasporas, and the Institution of Meditative Disciplines

Globalization has multiple facets: not only is the world interconnected by global capitalism controlled by multinational corporations located primarily in the West, but associated with it are global communications via television and the Internet and also, as Saskia Sassen (1998) says, with cities where the global economies have their "homes," these being places such as New York, London, Paris, Frankfort, Tokyo, and (perhaps) an emergent Bombay. Many theorists of globalization imagine that the global might undermine the local; or the local may persist within the frame of the global or deny that these processes are occurring; or that both accommodation and resistance are taking place (e.g., Featherstone 1990; Appadurai 1997; Amin 1997; Mittelman 2000). It seems to me that these theories are premature, largely because the future of global technologies cannot be predicted except very tentatively, and hence one cannot predict in any long-term fashion the world into which they exert their power, as Karl Popper (1961) noted some time back. Further, and more important, as Max Weber (1949) suggested, human beings must give meaning to their existence and respond to the threat of the homogenization of the world, though the development of global economic rationality might itself pose problems of meaning that people might resolve in multiple ways. There are those such as Jean Baudrillard (1975, 1997) who see modern communications occurring within globalization as part of a postmodern field. But the postmodern idealization of the fractioning of the world and the emergence of multiple cultures and the constant movement of signifiers without stable significations (signified) can be seen as a new form of romanticism for giving meaning to the seemingly meaningless world of our times.

In order to speculate on how these random thoughts relate to Buddhism, let me continue my narrative of the Theosophical Society. Even during the lifetimes of Olcott and Blavatsky, the movement began to be selectively indigenized in several of the societies of South and Southeast Asia. For example, Laurie Sears (1996) has convincingly shown that scholars such as Clifford Geertz might have misinterpreted the Javanese mysticism of the shadow theater, especially its purported Indic origins in texts like the Bhagavad Gita, when it probably was influenced by Dutch Theosophy via its impact on the cultural life of Javanese elites. In Sri Lanka the Buddhist Theosophical Society functioned primarily in the field of education; the actual takeover of the new Buddhist renaissance was the work of Anagarika Dharmapala, who was once a disciple of Olcott and later his foe. For Dharmapala, Buddhism was not only a movement of spiritual reawakening but also a nationalist and antiimperialist one. Since Dharmapala's work is well known, I shall only sum up his achievement in both the ecumenical and the nationalist level, that is, as the two forms of *sasanization* (Obeyesekere, 1972, 1976, 1995; Seneviratne, 1999).

For Dharmapala, Buddhism, divested of superstitious elements, had to be restored in the land of its origin and introduced into other Buddhist nations, much in line with Olcott's thinking. Olcott, however, had no sympathy whatever for the nationalist (and sometimes horrendously jingoistic) stance of Dharmapala. Yet from his own perception, Dharmapala's twin goals were not contradictory. Thus he continued his ecumenical work, particularly through the Mahabodhi Society he founded and its associated journal. Dharmapala also had a profound impact during the World Parliament of Religions in Chicago in 1893, as did the Vedantic reformer Vivekananda. Here Dharmapala made the point that Buddhism was consonant with evolutionary theory and the "law of cause and effect," and it "condemns the idea of a creator." Yet he placated his Western audience by saying that Buddhism did after all posit the idea of a "supreme God who is all love, all merciful, all gentle, and looks upon all beings with equanimity" and who accepts the cosmos as "a continuous process of unfolding itself in obedience to natural laws"; and he added: "to guide humanity in the right path a Tathagata (Messiah) appears from time to time" (quoted in Verhoeven 1998:213; Prebish, 1979; Williams and Queen, 1999). Dharmapala also asserted a year later that "Christ is a Buddha of a later time" (quoted in Verhoeven 1998:222). If Dharmapala produced a rational Protestant Buddhism consonant with European rationality and capitalism (which he idealized), Vivekananda did the same for Hinduism by transforming Ramakrishna's passionate and ecstatic Tantric-based religiosity and devotional worship of Kali into the neo-Vedantic rationalized Hinduism that has become the standard ideology of the various Ramakrishna missions that he founded and are now scattered in most European nations (Kripal, 1995; Kakar, 1991). Neo-Vedanta has become the orthodoxy of most Hindu immigrants and Western converts to Hinduism (though the latter do not practice the popular devotionalism and Brahmanical calendrical rituals obligatory for Hindu immigrants).

A similar situation seems to occur in the post-Dharmapala transplantation of various forms of Buddhism among immigrant communities that have come to Europe and the United States for employment in the globalizing economy. Unlike transmigrants to the Middle East who will eventually return home, the Asian Buddhists in the West are a permanent group. For them, Buddhism is a way of retaining their core cultural identity and resisting being swallowed by the homogenizing processes of globalization and the powerful presence of Christian churches in their midst. They, too, practice a purified or Protestant form of Buddhism in the wake of Olcott and Dharmapala, but they also worship the Buddha (if not the Hindu deities assimilated into popular Buddhism) and continue to practice Buddhist rituals and offer alms to monks. As with their home bases, meditation is a rare practice, though it is becoming increasingly popular owing to its acceptance by Euro-Buddhists. Thus immigrant Buddhism is *primarily* in terms of the local meanings of *sāsana* as the religion of one's homeland. Indeed, this was so with Dharmapala, if not Vivekananda. The passion and commitment that drove Dharmapala's ecumenicism is not that of the early Buddhist missions. Rather, it was national pride in his religion, his passionate hostility to the Christian missions, and his anti-imperialist stance that provided the dynamo that drove his ecumenical zeal. His hostility to the ethnic Tamils and Muslims in Sri Lanka paralleled a hostility to Hinduism that had supplanted Buddhism in the land of its birth. The two meanings of *sāsana* I mentioned earlier coexisted in the work of Dharmapala and on occasion were fused as they are today to a lesser degree in the many ethnic Buddhist temples in the West. To put it differently: the religion and politics of the home countries are very much alive (even more intensely so) in the adopted nations of immigrants, and the Buddhist temples constitute their base. It is therefore not surprising that when the British started their own "Euro-rationalized" Theravada temples, they had little appeal to Asian immigrant Buddhists in Britain.

Yet, what connects indigenous Buddhists with Euro-Buddhists (Buddhists of European descent) is in fact meditation, even though few Buddhists anywhere traditionally practiced it with any seriousness. One of the striking features of the contemporary global scene is the rapid spread of meditational practices among the lay intelligentsia, not only in today's Buddhist nations but also among Euro-Buddhists. Meditation is the royal road to salvation in Buddhism, and it is no accident that it is this feature that has spread globally in recent times, particularly after the 1960s and more spectacularly after the Tibetan diaspora to the West. Buddhist "insight meditation" is known as *vipassana* (Pali) or *vipaśyana* (Sanskrit), which attempts to diagnose the human condition, to recognize the illusory nature of the Self and sometimes all structures of existence, nirvana included. It is intrinsically related to Buddhist existential understandings of the world, especially the Four Noble Truths and the ultimate achievement of nirvana along with the cessation of rebirth. Calming meditation known as *samatha*, found in other religious traditions also, is at best a preliminary to the more arduous path of *vipassana*, which requires extraordinarily difficult exercises and the help of a "spiritual guide" or "true friend" so that the meditator can overcome the terrors of the fantastic. All Buddhist systems entail some form of *vipassana* with the possible exception of the two major forms of Zen. Yet virtually all forms of Euro-Buddhist meditation, including those of the middle-class Asians, is a much more shortened, communally oriented retreat, in the double sense of that term, from the labors of modern society.

The earliest attempt to modernize meditation was the work of the Burmese monk Bhikkhu Sadayaw, who invented a form of Buddhist meditation that dispensed with the preliminaries of calming (*samatha*) and produced a rationalized technology of *vipassana* divested of devotional practices, Buddhist cosmological understandings, as well as many doctrinal underpinnings. In a further radical move he said that monks were not necessary for teaching *vipassana*; and indeed non-Buddhists might also benefit from it—moves that touched the heart of modernity. One of Sadayaw's pupils from Sri Lanka founded a Buddhist meditation at Kanduboda, which provided meditation courses in English and also formal certification

(Gombrich and Obeyesekere 1988:238–39). Another extremely influential figure was John Kornfield, who trained Americans as *vipassana* instructors in Goenka meditation; in 1981 Kornfield founded Spirit Rock in Calfornia, where nine of the regular teachers are trained psychotherapists (Fronsdal 1998:170). I have already mentioned Goenka, who radically shortened Sadayaw's arduous three-month program to ten-day retreats (sometimes longer, but not more that thirty days). Goenka came from a wealthy Indian business family, and his techniques not only gained ground among educated native Buddhists but also spread very fast among Euro-Buddhists (Fronsdal 1998:166-67; Epstein, 1995; Molino, 1998). Perhaps most impressively, they were introduced to the newly emergent Theravada community of Newaris in Vajrayana Nepal. Goenka meditation is available on videocassettes, and presumably one can practice it without the guidance of a teacher. But it is not just Goenka who produces short-cut *vipassana* sessions; all Buddhist groups do, including Tibetan and other forms of Mahayana. Zen, the most popular form of Buddhist meditation in the United States, has always been short, based as it is on sudden illumination (satori). It seems to me that here we touch on an important feature of Buddhist meditation that can have a decided impact on the world. It is possible, and indeed may be happening this very moment, to introduce these revised meditational techniques not just through video but almost certainly via the Internet. In this sense one might say that Buddhist meditation has the prospect of becoming available globally such that one might begin to imagine Buddhism as a "world religion," not a popular one, but one that might eventually have small numbers of educated aspirants in virtually every nation under the sun.

✳

Buddhist Meditation and Rationality in a Global Economy

Because I have concentrated on meditation, I have had to ignore the impact of Buddhism on New Age religions. Buddhist meditational techniques entered Europe and America only after the 1970s, especially with the large presence of Asian refugees in those areas. The distinguished Weber scholar Detlef Kantowsky, himself a Buddhist, ironically comments that one does not need to go to Lhasa nowadays because "Lhasa really is everywhere today!" (Kantowsky 1995:101). And there is the visible presence of the charismatic Dalai Lama, who conducts weeklong meditative retreats in different parts of Euro-America. What are the reasons for Buddhism's appeal? According to Kantowsky, "the optimism of the Western rational enlightenment has been so thoroughly discredited that it is no longer able to justify man's subjection of nature: the arrogant cosmology which held that we could divorce ourselves from the rest of the world, cultivate it as a resource, or subject and fight it as a rival, is now bearing fruit" (102)—though not of a pleasant kind. And these trends are only accelerated in global capitalism's discontents documented by Saskia Sassen (1998), fostered by the amoral accumulation of wealth and the greed of the contemporary market, which in turn produces a further reification of the Self—all of which Buddhism diagnoses rather well in its idea that desire, greed, or attachment is the source of the unsatisfactoriness of the world. But to me this is merely the spur that the clear spirit might raise; it does show Buddhism as an alternative, nondestructive model for contemporary living, but it does not answer the question, Why Buddhist *meditation*?

To answer this question in an admittedly speculative manner, I would like to go back to a powerful nineteenth-century thinker who questioned Enlightenment rationality, scoffed at mainline reifiers of reason from Socrates and Plato to Kant, and, like Buddhists, pointed out the falsity of the Self and the entrenched Western idea that the limits of language are the limits of thought. I am, of course, looking at Friedrich Nietzsche, but not a relativist or postmodern Nietzsche, but rather the Nietzsche who formulated very early the opposition between Dionysian and Apollonian, an idealistic distinction that he maintained to the very end of his life. The two oppositions were reconciled in the past in the best of Greek tragedy, though most of the time they remained split.

Yet I think there is a problem here: Nietzsche and many modern and postmodern thinkers are critical of the Enlightenment project and its iron cage of rationality. Yet, can one living in the modern West escape from rationality's bondage or, to put it in early Nietzschean language, "pierce the veil of maya"? For Nietzsche the Dionysian in his ecstatic "entrancement" or "intoxication" can do it because his work is "an annihilation of the usual borders and limits of existence" (Nietzsche [1872] 2000: 46). "Something supernatural sounds forth from him: he feels himself a god, now he himself strides forth as enraptured and uplifted as he saw the gods stride forth in dreams. . . . Man is no longer the artist, he has become the work of art . . . in the shudder of intoxication" (Nietzsche 2000: 23). But it is one thing to sketch a lost past as Nietzsche does in *The Birth of Tragedy* or to imagine a powerful figure like Zarathustra as the Dionysian model prophet of the future who can cry out, "But I say unto you: one must have chaos in oneself to be able to give birth to a dancing star" (Nietzsche [1883] 1978:17). It is another thing to *be* Zarathustra, to incorporate him into one's own being; worse still to be able to create such things as visions and ecstatic trances in the field of modernity even for those who have intellectually rejected Cartesian rationality and the primacy of the Ego. Of course, art and music are expressions of the sublime, "the acre of green grass" that Yeats spoke of. And one can reenchant the outside world in many ways as, for instance, the European romantics did, but what about "inner experience," to use Georges Bataille's (1998) phrase? How can one *become* the living artist, if indeed the living artist as the ideal of a mode of living is not itself an illusion?

Most of us are caught up in Claude Lévi-Strauss's structuralist dilemma: Lévi-Strauss rejected the agency of the Ego, yet his work is in the true spirit of science; it is Apollonian in the narrowest sense because it is without the benefit of living in the "magic mountain," the domain of Apollo who was also the god of the Delphic oracle (Nietzsche [1872] 2000: 28). Apollonian thought is consonant with reason and moderation, but it is not consonant with Enlightenment rationality, which cannot tolerate any cultivation of a magic garden or an enchanted world.

Dilemmas similar to Lévi-Strauss's present themselves in many of the great figures of our time: Heidegger wanted to create, like Nietzsche himself, an authentic mode of existence or *dasein*; but it led him tortuously into the blind alley of fascism, a perilous land into which Nietzsche himself came close to trespassing. Wittgenstein passionately defended Saint Augustine; he himself periodically lived in isolation very much like a medieval mystic, but he was too much of an abstract thinker ever to be able to become someone like Augustine. Yet even those poststructuralist thinkers who protest against the rationality of the Enlightenment end up as prisoners of rationality. Foucault is the prime example of an antirationalist rationalist who tried to "pierce the veil of maya" in his own personal life—through sexuality, through the ingestion of hallucinatory drugs, through the visceral life of San Francisco's gay bars. Even the picture-thinking of surreal painters is close to the visuality of hysterical patients and the pictorial thinking of dreams, rather than to Buddhist meditative trance or Nietzsche's imagined Dionysianism. Except in rare instances, trance and vision continue to be relegated to psychosis in today's world. There is no way that one can be a modern or postmodern European living in the global economy and achieve a mode of being or nonbeing that one associates with visionary trance, Apollonian or Dionysian, and yet remain sane.

There is, however, at least one exception: and that is the Buddhist meditative askesis, a mode of nonbeing that can coexist with rationality though not in the same space-time. Why so? Because all forms of Buddhist meditation must eschew language and discursive reason for true understanding to develop, ideas that are hostile to rationality and science as commonly understood. Yet a modern Buddhist meditator can hark back to the world of discursive reason after the space-time of meditation is over, better equipped, he would say, to deal critically with that world. Buddhist meditation also has a complex disciplinary technology exemplified in Buddhaghosa's *Path of Purification*; but it is a technology that can be drastically modified and adapted in varying ways to modern life, sometimes in ways disturbing to those of us familiar with the history of Buddhism.

Yet whatever the form of meditation that one adopts from among the various forms of *vipassana* or Zen, it is Buddhist meditation and not Nietzschean Dionysianism, Buddhists could claim, that can "pierce the veil of maya," that illusory world of becoming or *saṃsāra* in which human beings are entangled but without the necessity for reifying the principle of individuality or sense of Self or Being which Nietzsche's Apollo exemplified. No wonder its appeal to educated, middle-class intellectuals discontented with the world of increasing globalization, allowing one to combine Dionysian rejection of the Self and retain Apollo's commitment to reason and moderation and yet live in the magic mountain, for a while at least, through meditation's askeses.

7 ✶ African Religion

JACOB OLUPONA

The global dimensions of African religion sweep across the plains of the African continent and into the African diaspora. Contemporary "African religion" is itself a product of globalization, for it is less a single tradition than a sociological context in which the elements of a variety of indigenous religious experiences are combined with Islam and Christianity. All three of these dimensions—indigenous religion, Africanized Islam, and Africanized Christianity—are part of the interactive, globalized African religious experience.

Some of the products of this growing interconnectedness of African and Africanized religions are new religions. But as Max Weber has observed, the charismatic becomes routinized, and new faiths eventually become accepted as established traditions. Following Ernst Troeltsch's categories, a breakaway sect can be characterized by the presence of doctrinal or ritual differences among the church's membership, and the new African religions have elements of both. These new religious structures reflect emerging values and the adoption of new practices in a changing social context. In the case of the African religions, this process reflects a growing pluralism among African religious institutions.

As globalization affects African religion both within Africa and throughout the African diaspora, new identities emerge. In the African Christian church, the Islamic mosque, and the Santeria temple, a new pluralism in African identity links the values, memories, and civil associations of a variety of African worldviews and moral systems. These are affected by their interactions with each other and with the cultures of the Western world.

The very language we use to describe the diverse religious experiences of people of African origin and descent is not only recent but also heavily dependent on non-African paradigms and Eurocentric views. Terms such as Africa, Black, and Pan-Africa all derive from recent conceptual periods in history, where parts of the geographic area we now so readily call Africa interacted with Europe. It is this interaction, beginning with trade and followed by the latter horrors of slavery and colonialism, that led to the Eurocentric idea of African religious cultures and worldviews.

As a consequence, it is difficult to come up with a distinct notion of African religion that is independent of the shaping tendencies of the paradigms and terms of the Western world. A truly indigenous understanding must include not only the history of Africa before colonialism but also aspects of living African communities that have derived from diverse heritages. Although the effort to define African religion can be challenging, a number of scholars, writers, and theologians have made the attempt. Writers associated with the Pan-African movement, for instance, which dates back for over three centuries, have sought to refine their sense of common being by looking at the totality of African religions within the global environment.

※

Globalization

In looking at the relationship between African religion and globalization, we should not assume that globalization is an inevitable force that will one day replace all traditional values within the world with one common consumerist mass culture. In Africa globalization has had a significant impact on traditions and cultural values, but at the same time African traditionalism retains a resiliency and adaptability that enables it to maintain cohesion both in non-

Western environments and in the context of faiths such as Christianity and Islam.

African traditions are adaptable. Instead of offering inflexible dogmatic beliefs, often they provide frameworks for viewing and processing information. If a new piece of information does not fit an existing framework, it can be modified but not necessarily rejected from the framework. For example, a form of taboo observed by an African people can be maintained until the old framework adapts, and it changes. What is interesting to ask about African immigrant religions is not so much what aspects of their traditions have been abandoned but how the frameworks of the traditions have adapted.

An interesting case in point is the changing role of women within African religious communities. Such women are commonly expected to preserve culture and traditions. As a consequence, a significant proportion of African church members are women. Yet these largely female congregations demonstrate a wide variety of attitudes toward the participation of women, from very limited to active leadership roles.

Another impact of globalization on African religion affects the nature of African civil societies. Both within Africa and worldwide, African religious institutions serve as a source of identity and legitimacy. Across Africa, religious leaders have challenged authoritarian and dictatorial political and military leaders such as the Abacha military dictatorship in Nigeria and in Moi's Kenya. During South Africa's apartheid era, the church played a critical role in racial reconciliation, and more recently Bishop Desmond Tutu chaired a committee on reconciliation. Within the African diaspora, African religious communities have actively participated in the social life of their communities as well.

✴

African Christianity

In describing African religion, we have to include the versions of Christianity and Islam that interact with traditional forms of African religion. Christianity in Africa is authentically African, but it is also global in that it is found in various forms in African communities in Africa, Europe, and the Americas. It is diverse not only in its geography but also in its three main strands: the African independent church movement, charismatic or Pentecostal churches, and the mission or mainline churches.

✳

African Independent Churches

African independent churches include the Celestial Church of Christ, Christ Apostic Church, and Cherubim and Seraphim in West Africa, Zulu Zionist churches in South Africa, and the Simon Kimbanque church in Zaire. These churches reflect the nexus between African indigenous beliefs and Christianity. Converts to Christianity in Africa, like those in Latin America, retain significant aspects of indigenous culture. Many of the first mission converts were socially marginal members of their communities who, with the rise of colonialism, became the new local elites. The social dominance of these African Christian elites led to the emergence of new religious rebels: new spiritual leaders who claimed they had been called by God to begin authentic African churches.

These new African leaders relied on both Christian and indigenous traditions as the source of truth and authority. Thus the African independent church retained aspects of indigenous tradition and belief. Christian images of divine leadership, the Holy Spirit, and faith healing, for example, were integrated into African ideas of community, ancestor worship, and revelation. Moreover, individuals could engage in a form of religious pluralism by participating in Christian and indigenous traditions at the same time, combining aspects of both. A naming ceremony, for example, could be utilized to incorporate significant aspects of indigenous and traditional beliefs. Hymns in African languages incorporated indigenous sayings and values. Special Africanized church services were created to supplement existing English sermons.

These syncretic processes, however, were not coordinated with one another, and the African independent church movement was often divided. To some extent these churches were separated from other African churches. They had difficulty in expanding their efforts beyond their original ethnic base. They were plagued with many of the same ethnic and political divisions that have separated the wider African society and created a series of contemporary political crises.

African Pentecostal or Charismatic Churches

African Pentecostal or charismatic churches are a rapidly growing sector of the African Christian communities. Unlike the African independent churches, which incorporate elements of indigenous African tradition, the charismatic church reflects the values of modernity, including Western rationalism and scientific and logical reasoning. Aspects of African spirituality such as divination, witchcraft, and polytheistic beliefs are strongly discouraged and are even portrayed as a product of the devil's influence. Yet these same churches often tolerate spirit possession as consistent with the Pentecostal tradition of "speaking in tongues." Pentecostal or "born-again" styles of worship are prominent in African immigrant communities, as well as in Africa itself.

Charismatic churches place a strong emphasis on the reality of the devil, a concept that is defined in a variety of ways among African societies. Concern about the devil leads to the importance of exorcism and the practice of deliverance by the Holy Spirit. In some ways these practices—and such elements of Pentecostal spirituality as fervent prayer, pragmaticsm, and proximate salvation—are close to African styles of spirituality. Yet "born-again" adherents in fact give very little recognition to the values of African indigenous traditions, and they critique traditional African beliefs as evil, superstitious, and contrary to the teachings of Christianity.

Mainline Mission Churches

The European and American mission church denominations remain the largest and the most organized churches in Africa, in spite of the recent upsurge of the Pentecostal-Charismatic communities. The Methodist Church, for example, boasts many centuries of presence in Africa. Though patterned after their mother churches abroad, the mission churches have adapted to their local situations. The 1960s—a time when most African nations became independent—were a watershed in the social history of these denominations, for they began to put in place innovations adapting their European practices to African spiritual sensibilities. More recently they have had to adapt to the increasing popularity of Charismatic-

Pentecostalism in the African scene. A number of mainline mission churches have adopted charismatic services as a way of preventing their youth from abandoning the churches as they did in the 1960s and 1970s when the mission churches lost a sizable number of their congregations to the African independent church movement.

Loyalties to mainstream mission church identities persist in the diaspora communities of African immigrants in America and Europe. Episcopal, Baptist, and Catholic churches increasingly offer services that reflect the interests and concerns of these immigrant communities. Churches in the United States have developed "ethnic ministries" that minister to a wide range of immigrant communities, including Africans. Among their accommodations are the use of African languages in hymns. The churches sometimes conduct services entirely in African languages. Often these services are held on Saturday or Sunday evenings in addition to the Sunday morning services. Since not all Africans speak the same language, only where there are significant concentrations of such African-language speakers as Igbo, Yoruba, or certain Ghanaian and Ethiopian communities will special-language services be provided.

Accompanying the rise of ethnic and national congregations in Europe and America is the increasing number of African clergy ministering solely to African congregations. Such priests and ministers are found especially in the Catholic Church, with a growing number in Episcopal, Anglican, and Methodist mainstream churches as well. These priests offer evidence that Africa has become a global center of Christianity and is able to send its own missionaries abroad.

✳

African Islam

The second heritage of African religion is the global faith of Islam. Unlike Christianity, which entered Africa primarily as a conduit for the disavowed and outcasts of African communities, Islam came to Africa as a religion of trade and commerce. Its pragmatism, scholarship, and globalizing linkages encouraged the development of vast trade empires across North Africa throughout the Middle Ages. Since no Muslim could become a slave, many Africans converted to Islam for protection as well as advancement.

Sub-Saharan Africa encapsulates the history of Islam, especially its contribution to knowledge, politics, and culture. The history of the western Sudanese empires of Ghana, Mali, and Songhi remains the most coveted phase of African history. Mali and Senegal, especially, were great centers of Islamic culture and intellectual discourse. The ancient cities of Timbuktu, Gao, and Genne, which maintained close links with the Mediterranean world, were centers of Islamic education, science, and culture.

At the same time, Islam contributed greatly to the growth of East African civilization, especially along the coastal region, where trade with the Arab world flourished. One result of this was the development of such linguistic cultures as the Swahili (based on a synthesis of Arabic and Bantu languages); another was the growth of maritime commerce long before colonialism entered the region.

Islam, like Christianity, has been able to adapt, capitalize on, and even exploit the technologies of modernity in favor of expanding its own faith as a global religion. Like African Christianity, the growing presence of expatriate African Muslims worldwide has begun to alter many of the largest cities in the Afro-Atlantic world. In London, New York, Washington, D.C., and Atlanta, Ghanaian Islamic communities are becoming prominent. Mosques in these cities that were once dominated by Arab and Pakistani communities are now beginning to witness a strong influx of Islamic Africans from West Africa. Within these African Muslim communities abroad, however, divisions based on ethnic and traditional origins remain.

[*]

African Indigenous Traditions and Faiths

Globalization takes on a slightly different form when it comes to indigenous African religions. Although the vast majority of Africans are Christian or Muslim, those who are followers of indigenous faiths have had a disproportionate impact abroad. Globalization has also become a powerful impetus in the worldwide expansion of African traditions such as the Yoruba faith of Ile-Ife and Oyo in Nigeria, and as the Fon in the republic of Benin. These variant forms of African traditions share many of the core beliefs of their African predecessors, but their indigenous nature has been masked as they have been adapted to Christianity.

Yoruba religion, expressed in Afro-Cuban Santeria, Afro-Brazilian Candomble, Shango tradition in Trinidad, and to some extent Vodou in Haiti, continues to refashion the culture and religious landscape of the New World. In the United States, the Yoruba-derived Orisha tradition is becoming an alternative devotional practice for thousands of Africans and even a growing number of Europeans and European Americans. This rich tradition has for over a century been the subject of scholarship in several fields: the humanities and social sciences; African, Caribbean, and American religious studies; and artistic and literary creativity and criticism. The steady stream of scholarly and popular works on Yoruba religion—both as it is practiced in West Africa and as it influences the African-based religions of the New World—suggests that this religion especially can no longer be viewed as a local ethnic tradition but as one that has in many ways attained the status of a world religion.

This globalization of African religious traditions embraces both African immigrants and Caucasian and Latino converts. They retain ties to Africa by importing priests such as Nigerian Yoruba-Ifa holy men. Indeed, a sizable number of Ifa priests have developed a strong clientele and semipermanent homes in many of America's largest cities.

In some cases African immigrant religion intersects with African American culture. African immigrants have helped to revitalize African indigenous religion in black American communities. Some of these communities have formulated a mythic linkage with traditions such as the Yoruba kingdom of Oyo or the cities of Ile-Ife, and communicate regularly with these cultural centers for the purpose of expanding and reinforcing these traditions within American society. A major American center for this revitalization is the Yoruba community of the Oyotungi Village in South Carolina, whose leader and oba (king), Oseijami Adefunmi I, has created a pan-African–U.S. traditional Orisha society. These Orisha devotees regularly visit Nigeria during the Ifa and Oshun festivals, and through their financial support they help to maintain cultural practices that are in decline in Africa itself.

❋

African Civil Religion

The fourth category of African religion is a trend that can be loosely described as a kind of African "civil religion." Many traditional religious myths, rituals, and symbols have been embraced by secular institutions and leaders as a means of developing greater legitimacy for themselves within African societies. Many members of indigenous elites within Africa and throughout the African diaspora have adopted religious practices to enhance their political influence, taking on symbols that would link them with notions of sacred kingships, ritual power, and historical-mythic legitimation.

❋

Conclusion

The globalization of African religion, therefore, entails not only the death of African traditional values but also in many cases their expansion and promotion. This is the product of an innovative and somewhat unpredictable reshuffling of many of Africa's cultures, faiths, and traditions—which have become a force for change in both Western and non-Western societies. This is nowhere more evident than in the crosscurrents between contemporary religious communities in the Americas and the expansion of African religions within the African continent itself. These movements are sources of cultural continuity, stability, and authority, and they demonstrate the remarkable resiliency and strength of character of African cultures. They have also at times been sources of tension, division, and conflict. These characteristics of innovation and diversity will continue to evolve as African religions expand from their roots in the three pivotal traditions of Christianity, Islam, and indigenous faiths.

8 ✳ Local Religious Societies

JUHA PENTIKÄINEN

Globalization has affected indigenous peoples and their traditional cultures in significant ways. Throughout the world, some 200 million people are identified by their religious cultures that are variously known as "native," indigenous," "local," and "ethnic" religions. They are the native people of North and South America, Siberia, and northern Europe and the tribal peoples of Africa, India, central Asia, Southeast Asia, Australia, New Zealand, and the Pacific Islands. If these people were members of a single religious community, it would constitute the sixth largest in the world. In an era of globalization, great numbers of these people have been obliged to leave their rural home territories to live in urban milieus or to migrate as emigrants or refugees to foreign countries, where they live in new environments in newly established groups and with strange neighbors. Globalization—with its universally disseminated flow of information and complicated economic and sociocultural structures—has both created a global family network and caused threats to traditional cultural values.

This global diaspora of native peoples greatly affects their religious life because their spirituality is ordinarily not conveyed through organizations and ideologies. Indeed, the languages of most indigenous peoples do not have any concept of religion in their vocabulary. In Siberia, for instance, the native people have the concept of *saman* instead. When I asked a Nanay shamaness from the Lower Amur Region in southeast Russia about the topic of religion, she replied, "Religion . . . ? It is Russian. We have our *samans* only." *Samans* are those "who know"—who are capable of shamanizing in shamanic cultures.

These are neglected traditions in the study of world religions. In general, there has been little knowledge of and interest in the great diversity of the "ethnic religions" to be found around the world—those typically that have no founder. During most of modern history, their map remained that of the gray area of territories of the unknown world, *terra hyperborea incognita*. It was considered the pagan world, a kind of no-man's-land with no religion, which for this reason could be conquered, missionized, and colonialized into the safe spheres of the Christian power structures of Western colonial domains.

※

Land and Language

These traditional cultures have been protected from such colonial assaults by their deep association with the land—with nature in general and with certain places in particular—and their maintenance of native languages. What is typical of the indigenous languages of the minority peoples of the Fourth World is their confrontation with Western ways of thinking and power mechanisms that overwhelmingly seem to overcome their local settlements, traditional ways of living, ecological environments, and languages.

Along the lines described by the anthropologist Robert Redfield, a division may be outlined between the "great," established religions of humankind and the "little" traditions—those that exist mainly in small local communities. The little religious traditions around the world are based on the memory of people of their local landscape, a natural or cultural place, a locality. This place becomes sacred when it is carried in the long, deep memory of an individual, a nuclear or extended family, a clan, an ethnic group or a people, or in some cases even a nation. Typically enough, borders and frontiers crossed by them have great significance in the narratives retaining that knowledge.

Arnold van Gennep, in his book *Les rites de passage* (1909; English translation, 1960), made an important observation about the significance of the territorial borders crossed by people when they migrate. These movements, in his opinion, follow a pattern: *séparation, marge, agrégation*. The same pattern is followed by the rites of passage related to social steps such as childbirth, naming, initiation, marriage, death. I want to emphasize the point of view that is usually forgotten in the functional and symbolic interpretations of van Gennep's theory focusing on the borderline between "this world" and "the other-worldly." Van Gennep, in my mind, was a prestructuralist interested in similarities between the procedures crossing frontiers and other territorial borders, rather than a functionalist dealing only with religious rites. The door is the boundary between the foreign and domestic worlds in the case of a temple; therefore, to cross the threshold is to unite oneself with a new world.

The meanings of locally based memory, as described in historical examples by Simon Schama (*Landscape and Memory*, 1996), are carried along as part of the inner mentality of people who flee or migrate. It acquires religious significance abroad in foreign milieus and is felt as a kind of sacred homeland, a hidden spot in the depths of the mind that cannot be expressed under threat or exile. The significance of this oral memory keeps up an identity of an ethnic religion, even after the community migrates to new milieus, surviving as an islet of a local "little" community, in Redfield's terms. It has repeatedly been recognized in refugee studies how native religious symbols have become strengthened under pressure, in refugee camps, even among people whose attitudes toward religion used to be hostile, alien, or indifferent in their home countries. Religiocultural symbols become manifest as the home altars of the emigrants and refugees wherever in the world people may have migrated or fled. The importance of religious rituals related to native rites of passage has also increased in diasporic immigrant communities. People who, of course, did not migrate or flee with an intention to die in a foreign country become interested in finding a spot of land on which to bury the departed members of the community, rather as an islet of their own if possible, as an important symbol of the locality of their religion.

Like location, language also is central to traditional cultures, though in many ways the spirituality of traditional peoples is their cultural mother tongue. Language conveys those spiritual meanings. In the last decade of the twentieth century, UNESCO launched a research program to report on the endangered languages in the world and to propose measures for supporting them. Such reports as *Arctic Languages, an Awakening* (1990) and *Endangered Languages* (1991) showed that the greatest threats concerned many small languages indigenous to the Arctic regions, due to the simultaneous ecological processes in the North. How one language dies while another survives is a question related to the ethnic and national processes that should be carefully studied in the contemporary world. This kind of comparative research is needed, since there is currently no comprehensive study on the special role of such native religio-national leaders as shamans in these processes. Field-based ethnographic research on contemporary shamans in Siberia, in Sápmi (Sami territories), and among the American Indian and Inuit peoples in the New World has produced phenomenologically interesting results on the roles of shamans in the survival processes of indigenous peoples.

Comparisons between the Sápmi or Sami people of Siberia and Mapuche Indian shamanism in Chile indicate how similar the worldwide problems of the indigenous peoples are. One key issue concerns their rights to the land and water resources they have occupied and used during the lives of tens of generations without marking it as their land property in the same way as the peoples who invaded their territories. The Sami national movement developed an internationally recognizable strength when its leaders were imprisoned as part of its battle against the occupation of the Alta River in northern Norway. Although the size of the Mapuche Indian population (approximately 1.2 million) is much greater than that of the Sami in the four countries in which they are found (Finland, Norway, Russia, Sweden); their cultural rights under Spanish rule have been even fewer.

The Ralco River as the ancient border between Mapuche and Spanish domains in Chile has at the turn of the third millennium become the symbol of the national battle of the Mapuche Indians. A dozen shamanic families have threatened to stay on their hills when the second dam is built at the Andes, even at the risk of being drowned by water. The processions of Indian demonstrators, who started from their holy mountains led by their native leader Sara Imilgei, were in January 2001 stopped by water tanks in front of the presidential palace in Santiago, Chile. In my interview with Imilgei, she said that their Andean gods would solve their problems. The gravestone of a Mapuche shaman stands as the religious symbol of national confrontation. It is located on the road leading to the dam builders' camp after its transfer was stopped by an accident that killed the truck driver who should have moved it away. The building project was temporarily closed during our field tour in January 2001 after a Mapuche cemetery was found on the hill of the Ralco River. Since the common interests of the national and ecological movements have found each other, the Ralco movement is nowadays called the Bio Bio project.

[*]

Worldwide Revival of Ethnic Religions

The diaspora of traditional native communities in new locations around the world has in many cases weakened these groups' identities, but it has also brought an awareness of the need to protect traditional places and languages. The globalization of culture also has made nonindigenous people aware that the native traditions are part of a world inheritance to be protected and appreciated by all. The year 1993 was celebrated as the United Nations year of the indigenous peoples around the world. The proclamation was, in the minds of the Fourth World political leaders, more a show of goodwill and symbolism than an effort to bring achievements and practical results, but it did help to increase the solidarity and togetherness of the indigenous peoples and to demonstrate that the different indigenous communities around the world had common concerns.

The election of Alejandro Toledo as the first native American Indian president of Peru in 2001 is an interesting indication of reformations taking place in Latin American countries. The inauguration of this learned economist, who still speaks his Ketsuan Indian language learned at the Andes, although he was educated at Harvard University and trained in the World Bank, was accompanied on July 29, 2001, by a sacred ceremony on Macchu Picchu's holy mountain, eyewitnessed by Prince Felipe of Spain, Israeli foreign minister Shimon Peres, and President Ricardo Lagos of Chile, among others. Toledo received a golden ax and necklaces from two barefoot priests after their plant and food sacrifice to Apui, the mountain god, and Panchamama, Mother Earth. Showing his loyalty to his native background shared by the clear Peru majority,

President Toledo said: "I have come to thank for the strength and energy Apui and the Earth have given to me." His speech was followed by a speech by his wife, an anthropologist of Belgian background, who said that the fortune and well-being of the ancient rulers will now return to Peru.

Russia, with its abundance of minority populations—over a hundred discrete communities—has after Soviet rule created a ministry for the problems of its indigenous peoples. Shamanism has accordingly been listed as a religion, and interest in its value as an example of cultural heritage has increased. In my fieldwork in this region since 1988, I found that traditional shamanism has survived after the persecutions of Soviet exile. Among the Khanty, the Yakut, and the Mandchu Tungusic peoples at the very cradle of shamanism, the vocabulary of a network of native shamanic concepts has been retained. In central Siberia, such republics as Sakha (Yakutia), Khakassia, Buryatia, and Tuva have proclaimed shamans as the bearers of their cultural traditions. They support the official organizations of registered shamans who practice in their shamanic clinics, as do shamans in contemporary Korea and China as well.

How and why such an archaic phenomenon as shamanism has overcome the pressures of the great ideological, religious, and ecological changes that have taken place in the twentieth century in various territories and cultures is an interesting target of research waiting to be more fully explored. Native traditions have endured despite the influence of modern ideologies, the pressures of urbanization, collectivization, and other forms of social change, and the ravages of oil, military, and other modern intrusions. Despite these impacts on their ethnic cultures and the ecological environment of their homelands, these people have survived. The fieldwork carried out in these regions will provide evidence of the importance of the role of shamans and other traditional leaders in the ethnic revival and survival processes of the indigenous peoples. Shamans have been persecuted for ideological and religious reasons in their respective countries. Some of those who survived have become remarkable ethnic and national leaders, giving new meaning to their traditional authority roles and strengthening the revitalization processes of their peoples.

II ✳ *Religion in a Global Age*

9 ❊ Religion in Global Perspective

MARTIN RIESEBRODT

In recent decades the dramatic global resurgence of religious movements—many of them fundamentalist—has caught many people by surprise. Most of us believed that such a resurgence of religion was not possible, since, according to our modernization myth, we were to expect a continuous universal trend toward the secularization and privatization of religion. There were several options for the fate of religion in the modern world, but neither a return of religion as a public force nor its ability to shape people according to its own ethos or habitus was among them.

Certainly, very few people expected religion to totally disappear. Most assigned it to a legitimate space in the private sphere and assumed that religious institutions would undergo a process of internal secularization and would increasingly adapt to the requirements of modern structures while maintaining their religious symbolism. Some imagined that national ideologies or civil religions would functionally replace religious traditions, or expected religious values to permeate modern societies, leaving behind the traditional forms of religion. But few were prepared for the global resurgence of religions as a public force and a powerful shaper of religious subjects.

The attempts of social theorists to cope with their own cognitive dissonance have been nearly as interesting as this surprising return of religion itself. The two most typical reactions were denial and instant conversion. Some authors have simply insisted that their expectations of modernization and secularization are basically sound. Focusing on the resurgence of religion outside the modern West allowed them to pretend that these revivals of religion are still part of a modernizing process. And, not surprisingly, many have taken pains to detect a "Puritan spirit" or an "inner-worldly asceticism" in such movements, revealing their misreading of Weber's "Protestant Ethic" thesis as a general theory of modernization.

Other authors have chosen the opposite route of instant conversion by denying any general trend toward secularization in the West and elsewhere. Rational choice theorists and their allies in particular have argued that secularization is just an effect of European-style religious monopolies. Wherever religious pluralism and competition have predominated, such as in the United States, secularization has not taken place. Here religion is—and always has been—alive and well.

Against these two positions I claim that neither a denial of the secularizing tendencies of Western modernity nor a blind belief in an irreversible universal trend toward secularization will do. On the one hand, the resurgence of religious movements and personal piety on a global scale has shed serious doubt on the secularization thesis. On the other hand, it would be ludicrous to deny that secularization in terms of processes of institutional differentiation has actually taken place. Modern states, including the United States, are widely secular. Neither capitalism and bureaucracy nor modern science and modern culture are based on or even compatible with religious principles. And since much of the religious resurgence is directed against modern secularism, one would actually misunderstand these movements unless one acknowledges secularization as a fact.

Therefore, instead of explaining away the apparent contradiction between processes of secularization and of religious resurgence, we should attempt to understand why these processes occur simultaneously and how they might be interrelated. Since conventional theories of religion have failed to provide us with a convincing explanation, this might be a good occasion to revisit them critically and to attempt to formulate a theory that makes better sense of religion in the modern world.

✳

Can One Theorize about Religion?

But is such a general theory of religion actually possible? The very concept of religion has been criticized recently. Some have argued that religions exhibit such a great diversity of beliefs, practices, and symbols that one cannot capture them in one definition; others have emphasized that "religion" is a Western invention the meaning of which is differently socially constituted at different times in history and across traditions. Moreover, such general definitions of religion have usually expressed ethnocentric Western views and normative claims in the disguise of universal truths.

Admittedly, many theories have been based on rather Eurocentric rationalist and normative models of cognitive progress, expectations of secularization and privatization of religion, as well as on a modern Western notion of the "self." Certainly, occidental parochialism is implicit in much of sociological and anthropological theorizing. However, this is not a necessary consequence of any general concept and theory of religion, but rather the result of specific definitions and theoretical perspectives. Moreover, the widespread use of the term "religion," even by authors who claim to reject it, suggests that a general concept like *religion* seems to be logically required whenever people are aware of a plurality of "religious" faiths and practices and make comparisons. Also the objection that religion is discursively constituted and therefore historically and culturally related is not very convincing, since this applies not just to religion but to any concept, like "gender," "class," "ethnicity," "genealogy," "medieval Christianity," or "Islam."

Since the usefulness of a general concept and theory of religion cannot be decided a priori, I will very briefly outline some basic elements of such a theory that is capable of explaining religious phenomena on a global scale despite obvious differences between religious traditions, great diversity within traditions, and historical transformations of traditions, bracketing for the moment the problematic notion of "tradition" itself. This requires as a first step the clarification of what is meant here by "religion" and by "theory."

I suspect that objections against attempts at conceptualizing and theorizing "religion" are often based on erroneous assumptions about the epistemological status of such an enterprise. Of course, "religion" is an analytical category that exists only as an intellectual construct. No one can believe in or practice "religion as such," and we can only observe culturally, socially, and historically definite religious practices. Moreover, a social scientific concept of religion is different from a theological or a legal one. Therefore, a sociological concept and theory of religion neither intends to capture any "essence" of religion nor to distinguish good from bad religion, or legitimate from illegitimate religion. It rather offers a systematization and explanation of phenomena defined as "religious" from a consciously chosen one-sided perspective based on a cross-culturally comparative analysis of processes of social action and interaction. The justification of this perspective should be based on historical relevance, theoretical consistency, and empirical validity. Obviously, the possibility exists that more than one theoretical perspective fulfills these requirements.

Moreover, it is equally legitimate to subsume phenomena defined by one approach as "religious" under conceptual and theoretical frames other than "religion," like ideology, knowledge, or discourse. For example, instead of theorizing "religion" universally, one could theorize the discourses through which different concepts of "religion" (or comparable terms) are produced. Such alternative theorizing has to meet the same criteria of relevance, consistency, and empirical validity. My own approach affirms the usefulness of the concept of religion but draws the following conclusions from the shortcomings of other theories.

First, a theory of religion should avoid any implicit or explicit value judgment about religious beliefs and practices. It should not rank them according to evolutionist or developmental schemes, higher or lower forms, good or bad religions. The problem of evolutionary perspectives is their obvious ideological design. They usually claim implicitly or explicitly either that Protestantism is the highest form of religion or that science is the highest form of knowledge. I have not met an evolutionist yet who constructed a scheme where he or she ended up in the middle or at the bottom.

Second, religion should be analyzed in terms of a relatively autonomous system of meaningful actions and interactions that is interconnected with other systems of practices but not their reflection. I will explain this concept later in more detail.

Third, a theory of religion should attempt to account for the subjective as well as the objective side of religion, the perspective from the individual social actor as well as from the institutional order.

Fourth, a theory of religion should account for the emotional as well as the cognitive aspects of religion. In their intentions and effects, religious practices, like other practices, are neither exclusively rational and instrumental nor exclusively irrational.

And finally, a theory of religion should pay attention to the content of religious beliefs and practices but should avoid homogenizing them into closed systems of traditions writ large. Any such essentialization of religious traditions implicitly favors "orthodoxy" and "orthopraxy" and often overlooks the internal pluralism and historical transformation of traditions. "Tradition" in its scientific use is an ideal type and as such has only a heuristic value. It is not meant to interpret and explain the empirical evidence but only provides us with a hypothetical model.

✳

The Methodological Priority of Practices

In order to formulate such a theoretical frame I propose to focus on religious practices. Unlike religious beliefs and experiences, religious practices lend themselves to empirical observation. Instead of first systematizing religious beliefs of a "culture," "tradition," or "society" and then interpreting religious practices as enactments of such beliefs, I propose an ideal-typical description of beliefs that are implied in practices. What is the difference?

The first approach puts the emphasis on a rich construction of worldviews, cosmologies, and complex symbol systems. This necessarily directs attention to those who have the broadest knowledge of religious beliefs and are able to articulate and systematize them: religious intellectuals and specialists or scholars who substitute for them. A deductive interpretation of practices as enacted beliefs, hence, becomes "theological" in its basic outlook. It reinforces distinctions between "high" and "popular" religion, sees ordinary practitioners as lacking the knowledge of the "real" meanings of their actions, and emphasizes particularistic features of religious traditions.

Starting from a model of religious practices and their implicit logic shifts our perspective. The actual practices of different groups and categories of people are seen as culturally and socially embedded meaningful actions. But these meanings are not assumed simply to be deficient versions or unconscious enactments of the "theologically correct" or the culturally most complex ones.

A model that constructs a logic of religious practices underlying their concrete culturally and socially shaped forms shifts the focus from intellectual metadiscourses to practitioners, from a "theological" to a "pragmatic" perspective. Such an approach overcomes the value judgments implicit in distinctions between "higher" and "lower" forms of religion (e.g., "popular" or "folk" religion) or "good" and "bad" religion (e.g., "magic," "superstition," "cult"). It treats the practitioners as competent actors and provides a theoretical frame that allows for generalizing as well as particularizing comparisons. This approach does not deny, however, that the reconstruction of complex worldviews has a heuristic value and that institutionalized meanings can shape the explicit and implicit motivations of religious practitioners, but it treats this as an empirical question.

✳

The Logic of Religious Practices

Religious practices can be distinguished from other kinds of social actions on the basis of three logically implied core assumptions: (1) there exist superhuman, extraordinary, "amazing," in modern Western terms generally "supernatural" personal or impersonal powers; (2) these powers control dimensions of human/social life that normal social actors cannot control directly by their own power; and (3) social actors are able to gain access to these powers. Depending on how these powers are imagined, one can influence or manipulate them, can communicate or exchange gifts and services with them. Or they can empower themselves beyond the ordinary through the internalization or internal activation, or through fusion with such powers.

These basic assumptions come to bear in the distinction between three types of religious practices: interventive, discursive, and derivative. *Interventive practices* engage in attempts at getting access to superhuman powers; communicating and exchanging gifts and services with them; manipulating them; or empowering oneself. Examples of such practices are sacrifices, prayers, spells, divinations, and ascetic and mystical disciplines.

Discursive practices engage in linguistic exchanges between social actors about the nature of superhuman powers and appropriate ways of interacting with them, manipulating them, or acquiring them. Such practices pass on, reinforce, interpret, and revise religious knowledge and, in conjunction with interventive practices, shape the ethos or habitus of social actors. Discursive practices are by no means restricted to intellectuals, such as theologians, but are common to all kinds of religious actors.

The concept of *derivative practices* refers to the religious shaping of social action where social actors expand their notions of religious significance and make their nonreligious practices conform to religious rules by committing acts that are believed to please the powers or produce blessings or by avoiding acts that are believed to anger the powers or effect misfortune.

All three types of practices are often only analytically separable, and even the same practice in the same context could be classified differently. For example, the reading of a sacred text could take on the meaning of a discursive practice but also that of an interventive practice. These different types of practices often occur simultaneously, mutually reinforce each other, and are equally involved in religious socialization and in the creation of "moods and motivations," as well as "conceptions of a general order of existence," as Clifford Geertz has aptly put it.

Whereas much attention has been paid in classical social theories to derivative practices, and in recent theories to discursive practices, this theory focuses on interventive practices. From the perspective employed by this proposed theory, discursive practices primarily serve as facilitators of interventive practices, while derivative practices are their effects. Accordingly, interventive practices represent the analytical core, and I will focus on them by turning to the question of why they are performed.

I argue that a common theme in interventive practices across traditions lies in their attempt to prevent crises from happening or to manage them when they have happened. The crises (or dangers, risks) addressed in such practices are found primarily in domains that could be classified in Western terms as nature, the human body, and social relations. With regard to nature, interventive practices refer primarily to phenomena that are beyond the routine technical control of a given society but are believed to pose a major threat. With regard to the human body, they refer mostly to its reproductive capabilities and mortality (e.g., fertility and birth, illness and death). With regard to society, interventive practices center on the precariousness of social relations, especially inequality, authority, conflict, changes in status, or crises of solidarity and identity.

Within interventive practices I distinguish between three types: routine, occasional, and virtuoso. *Routine practices* cultivate and affirm the exchange relationship between superhuman powers and social actors on a regular basis. They follow, for example, a daily, weekly, monthly, or yearly cycle. The more frequent ones tend to primarily maintain good relations, while the others may commemorate significant past events when the powers intervened in people's lives to help or punish them. Accordingly, routine practices honor the powers and express gratitude, hope, grief, or joy.

Occasional practices are linked to events that are not defined by the calender but rather follow the individual or the family life cycle. They are performed at the occasions of births, initiations, weddings, and deaths. They also take place in response to actual crises, like illness, catastrophes, and war.

Virtuoso practices seem to be different in motivation from both routine and occasional practices. But I think they can be interpreted as often attempting to overcome the conditions for the possibility of crises, dangers, risks, and suffering in principle, for example, through contemplative or ascetic disciplines. The self-empowerment through such practices often has the consequence of elevating virtuosi to the status of superhuman powers or mediators who themselves then become objects of interventive practices.

※

Culture: Profane and Religious

Obviously, the response to the challenges of crises does not have to be religious, since such experiences do not necessarily lead to the assumption of the existence of superhuman powers that control what we do not. As one could formulate with reference to Freud, other illusions are available. However, the universality of religious practices suggests that the conditions for the possibility of religion lie in shared features of the human species. As Peter Berger and others have argued, in the process of human evolution, instinctual regulation of social behavior has been increasingly replaced by ratiocination, communication, and interpretation. The lack of directedness through instincts has made it not only possible but also necessary for the human species to interact creatively with its natural environment and "invent" regulatory systems for social interaction. Humans are by biological necessity cultural beings who through social interaction and communication order their social relations cognitively, morally, and emotionally. Part of this process of culturalization of the human species is the development of "religion." Without exactly mirroring these evolutionary processes, the development of children shows certain parallels.

I propose to distinguish between religious and profane dimensions of culture in terms of an ideal-typical opposition between practices that contain a reference to superhuman powers and practices that lack such a reference. If culture in general refers to the cognitive, moral, and emotional repertoire of a given society through which practices are regulated, then the religious culture primarily refers to practices that are based on interactions with superhuman powers, and to discourses and symbolizations that reflect on the character and will of such powers, our relationship to them, and the appropriate methods of approaching or manipulating them. In contrast to profane culture, the religious repertoire contains, preserves, and cultivates the resources to cope with those dimensions of human life that are beyond routine social control and therefore are believed to require the intervention of superhuman powers.

Since human beings cannot but interpret their external and internal relationships, there is a special need for interpretation and explanation when confronted with one's own powerlessness, with lack of control, crises, or high risks. The cognitive need to understand and the emotional one to cope with these situations can be seen as two related modes of reassurance. Since the distinction between profane and religious culture is an ideal-typical one, its boundaries can be rather fluid. Moreover, those distinctions are not static. Profane practices can become sacralized, religious practices profanized.

[*]

The Logic of Religious Institutions

So far I have abstracted from institutional contexts to which I am turning now. What is the nature of religious institutions, and how are they interconnected with other social fields? Given the approach to religious practices I have taken, religious institutions can be defined as rules and norms that regulate the interaction between human beings and superhuman powers, the discourse about these powers, their nature, significance, and interventions into our lives, as well as the religious penetration of everyday life. Religious institutions tend to exhibit at least a rudimentary division of labor that ascribes to different categories of people certain inborn or acquired qualifications in terms of knowledge and skills for the performance of practices or the acquisition of religious knowledge, but the degree of this differentiation can vary immensely across history and traditions.

With increasing division of religious labor, religious institutions become more systematized, rationalized, and centralized and are transformed into religious organizations. Through these processes a permanent and stable system of religious inequality and authority is created, which often attempts to monopolize the means of "salvation" by controlling religious know-how, symbols, objects, and spaces, as well as the training and licensing of religious specialists. This enables religious organizations to expand their control over people and to accumulate wealth and power far beyond their mediating religious functions.

Nevertheless, it is important to analytically distinguish the authority of superhuman powers from the authority of religious institutions or organizations because the latter is derived from the acceptance of the former. To fuse these two dimensions means to buy into the ideology of religious organizations. The claim of religious organizations to legitimately, efficaciously, and often exclusively mediate between humans and superhuman powers may be rejected, whereas the authority of the superhuman powers themselves is not doubted, and alternative mediators may gain legitimacy. We deal here with two systems of authority that can be merged but also separated again.

Religious institutions are obviously interlinked with the profane culture, social structure, and institutional order. Already the definition and framing of a crisis tend to be informed by the degree to which a given society understands and controls its natural environment. And the imagination of superhuman powers is often shaped by social structures of authority. Moreover, religious organizations permanently interact with other systems of power and authority that are derived from the control of force and warfare, as well as the control of wealth, which may or may not be institutionally differentiated from each other. Here, again, I propose to not simply fuse these different dimensions into one block of power, authority, and wealth but to distinguish them analytically and determine their interrelatedness under concrete historical circumstances.

I propose to understand religion as a "relatively autonomous" social field. This implies that, on the one hand, religious practices and institutions cannot be adequately understood outside of their concrete social, historical, political, and economic context. But, on the other hand, they are not simply a reflection or symbolization of political or economic orders. Religions can have a rather ambiguous relation vis-à-vis political, economic, and even religious organizations. Since religions offer complex repertoires of beliefs and practices, they can be selectively instrumentalized not only for the legitimation of authority and privilege but also for their delegitimation and sometimes transformation. Moreover, religions also constitute—from the actors' point of view—a relatively autonomous field of communication and exchange with superhuman powers. Although these exchanges are related to the anticipation, experience, or management of crises that may originate in the social, political, or economic sphere, they also create their own internal logic and dynamics that may well be in competition or conflict with political and economic interests, as well as with the mediation offered by dominant religious organizations.

As this approach is suggesting, crises are the seedbed of religious work. This does not mean that people are or become "religious" only in moments when they experience crises. To the contrary, most religious practices are fully embedded in everyday social relations and are part of daily, weekly, and monthly routines. However, crises tend to add a dynamic dimension to religion. Religious beliefs and practices are invented, abolished, revitalized, and reinterpreted as reaction to perceived crises and may thereby confirm, reform, or even revolutionize social structures, institutional orders, and religious traditions. As long as traditional structures and practices of crisis prevention and management are seen as successful and beyond doubt, they are reaffirmed. Otherwise, new practices and cognitive orders may be created that revise how superhuman powers are imagined and how one can gain access to them. New modalities of interaction between human and superhuman beings may be institutionalized. New groups and categories of people may now qualify to access them directly or serve as mediators. And finally, the pragmatic effects of the communication between social actors and superhuman powers may be drastically revised. For example, religious specialists may be replaced by laypeople, priests by prophetic preachers, or sacrifices by ascetic or ethical practices.

The universality of religious beliefs, practices, and institutions suggests that humans have a limited ability to cope with extreme uncertainty. Historically, it has been mostly through religions that the chaotic potential of crises has been culturally transformed into the semblance of cosmos. Religions have created the trust in the ability of social groups to prevent crises from happening or to cope with them if they do happen. Religion as a resource of cultural crisis prevention and management, hence, equally serves collective and individual needs.

✳

Secularization and the Global Resurgence of Religion

What, now, are the advantages and consequences of this approach? First of all, the theory allows for a relatively clear distinction between religious and other kinds of practices. Unlike approaches that define religion in terms of a supposed function, phenomena such as rock concerts, football games, or shopping in a supermarket are not regarded as religious here. At the same time, religion is also not defined in terms of an "experience" that usually is neither empirically accessible nor universal. Such an emphasis on individual sensibilities excludes the rational, pragmatic, and institutional sides of religion. Instead, religion is defined as a specific type of meaningful social actions and interactions that can be equally theorized from the perspective of actors as from that of institutional orders.

Second, the approach directs our attention to religious practices on different levels of social aggregation—from "society" to intermediary groups to the individual—as well as to religious practices of different classes and categories of people. The emphasis shifts from seeing religion primarily from an "orthodox" and intellectualist perspective as a unified cognitive, moral, and practical system to seeing it as a field in which people of different class, gender, ethnicity, or age deal with their specific risks, crises, and experiences of powerlessness. This emphasis urges us not to be content with the fiction of a given "culture" or "society" as a whole but to theorize, study, and explain the specificity of religious practices of men and women, of people in different stages of their life cycle, of dominant and subordinate classes, status groups, and ethnic groups who make creative use of religious repertoires and attribute meanings to their practices with reference to shared institutions, symbols, and beliefs.

Finally, this approach allows us to make better sense of religion in the modern world. Initially, I have claimed that processes of secularization and of global resurgence of religion not only have taken place to various degrees but also are interrelated. From the perspective of this theory, secularization has occurred as a consequence of increasing human control and "world-mastery" and its institutionalization in separate social spheres. The massive growth of scientific knowledge and its practical application, most important in medicine, has vastly expanded human control over spheres of high risk and threat. The development of a welfare state has neutralized some of the major existential risks for the middle and lower classes. The replacement of monarchical and aristocratic systems of authority by democratic ones has disenchanted politics. Religious narratives of salvation history have in part been replaced by or fused with historical narratives of the nation. Bureaucratic principles of organization and the institutionalization of "efficiency" have widely removed religious ethics from the economy and politics. These processes have objectively weakened the relevance of religion in many respects and have widely restricted it to a separate sphere, primarily serving individual and private needs.

However, in part simultaneously, in part with some time lag, new dimensions of uncertainty, risk, and powerlessness have opened up. Science and technology not only have extended our control over nature but also have created new risks, like the threat of environmental catastrophes. Democratization has not just profaned politics; it has also reenchanted politics by enabling "charismatic" leaders to mobilize mass support. Capitalism not only has freed certain social groups and women from patriarchal bonds and given them new opportunities but also has enforced on them a mobility of nearly unprecedented scope. As a consequence, kinship relations have been dissolved and family structures destabilized, and people have been exposed to the uncertainties and irrationalities of the market.

Capitalism is a revolutionary force that permanently transforms social structures and promotes upward and downward social mobility, as well as geographic mobility. In particular, its recent global spread has simultaneously created wealth and poverty of immense proportions, dramatically undermining not only the economic standings of masses of people but also their social identities. To the degree that Western modernism could convincingly instill the belief in its ever-increasing ability to control nature, the human body, and society, religion receded. But the destabilizing effects of Western modernization have undercut such beliefs and paved the way for a resurgence of religious modes of crisis prevention and management. Seen from this theoretical perspective, secularization and the global resurgence of religion represent not a contradiction but rather two sides of the same coin.

Max Weber once suggested with respect to the ancient Near East and Greece that "epochs of strong prophetic propaganda" in all its different forms are related to "the reconstitution of the great world empires in Asia, and the resumption and intensification of international commerce" (*Sociology of Religion*, 48). These processes in the ancient world may exhibit some interesting parallels to what we presently like to call "globalization." Certainly, many of the contemporary revival movements, in particular "fundamentalist" ones, react to crises that can be characterized as effects of such dramatic economic and political transformation processes.

However, their reactions, like the ancient ones, are nevertheless specifically religious. Contemporary fundamentalist movements do not articulate a socioeconomic agenda nor organize as class movements; rather, they represent *cultural milieus* in the sense that their group identity and the perception of a common fate are defined primarily by shared ideals of a religiously grounded sociomoral order. These movements do not represent religious traditionalists but appropriate and reinterpret their traditions quite selectively and innovatively in the light of specifically modern experiences. Despite many differences between religious traditions, fundamentalist movements across traditions react to comparable social experiences and as a result develop similar countervisions of a better society. They all tend to unanimously demand the restoration of patriarchal principles of authority and morality, claiming that only such a return can solve the problems and crises of modernity.

Since secularism and religious revivalism constitute each other socially and ideologically, religious revivals neither represent the realization of the religious "essence" of any "civilization," nor are they momentary aberrations from a predestined path toward secularism, but they are and will remain a recurring historical phenomenon, even in the modern world.

10 ✷ *Antiglobal Religion*

ROLAND ROBERTSON

The destruction of the World Trade Center on September 11, 2001, indicates that America has become the target of a certain strand of antiglobal religion. The antiglobalization movement has both secular and religious dimensions. The events in Seattle surrounding—or, more accurately, opposing—the meeting of the World Trade Organization (WTO) in the fall of 1999 have been widely regarded as a turning point. They constituted a symbolic beginning of the targeting of the global. Seattle 1999 amplified a strong switch away from the adage "think globally, act locally." While such a turn from the half-local to the totally global was easy to recognize among long-standing students of what has come to be called globalization, in reality the adage "think globally, act locally" has had a life of its own until it was more or less exploded not merely by the events in Seattle but also by those subsequently in Washington, D.C.; Windsor, Canada (where protests were mounted against the Organization of American States); London and some other cities on May Day, 2000; Davos, Switzerland, in connection with meetings of the World Economic Forum; the fall 2000 demonstrations in Prague against the World Bank and the International Monetary Fund; and the agitation against the European Union summit in Nice in December 2000. Other protests against globalization and capitalism took place, inter alia, in 2000 in Biarritz and Seoul, and elsewhere in 2001 and later. Nearly, if not all, of these have involved mixtures of nationalities and of motives, a collage of peoples and intentions.

One might also mention the protests against McDonald's that rapidly developed in 2000 in France, following the "McLibel Trial" in London in the mid-1990s. Although French intellectuals are particularly well known for blaming the "Anglo-Saxons" (whoever might be meant by this term) for most of the world's problems, the United States of America is taken to be the primary locus of globalization, and thus McDonald's and a number of other supposedly U.S.-based corporations, such as Starbucks, the Gap, and Blockbuster, are portrayed as prominent and highly effective agents of globalization. I say supposedly because many corporations that are widely thought of as American are not in fact anywhere near as all-American, at least as far as their ownership is concerned, as they are often thought to be.

Of course McDonald's is often taken as the strongest symbol of global capitalism (cf. Ritzer 2000). But regardless of its actual, practical impact around the world, a crucial aspect of the academic attention to McDonald's is that it does, indeed, have an enormous symbolic significance. McDonald's represents the United States in a way that is rivaled only by Coca Cola and, in more recent years, Nike, Starbucks, and so on. Yet McDonald's claims to be highly respectful of local traditions and of cultural variety generally. And this is, to a degree, validated by Watson's edited book on McDonald's in East Asian capitals (Watson 1997), in which a number of anthropologists illustrate the argument that McDonald's facilitates *localization*. This phenomenon is part of the larger argument that much that is taken to be hegemonically homogenizing is, on closer inspection, actually the basis on which locality becomes more evident. This is, to put it all too simply, one of the ways in which the global produces the local.

Much of this overall activity concerns the forgiveness of Third World debt, in which religious participation has been strong. Particularly active in this process has been the organization called Jubilee 2000 that closed down at the end of 2000, to be replaced by Drop the Debt. But when the G7/8 meeting of industrialized economies was held in Genoa, Italy, in 2001, it took place in a country where agitation for forgiveness of Third World debt is considerable and has papal backing. In fact the role of the Roman Catholic Church in opposing economic globalization has been considerable in recent years. For, to the Catholic hierarchy and many lay Catholics, globalization represents the high point of capitalism, against which the church throughout the twentieth century expressed much opposition. The present pope has, in fact, spoken vividly against globalization in recent years—but the present author's impression is that even though the ostensible target of papal complaint has been against global capitalism, there is considerable concern in the Vatican about the ways in which what is commonly called globalization (in the broad sense) is challenging the worldwide presence of Catholicism as the most powerful and influential "world religion." Or, to put this differently, (Roman) Catholicism has for many centuries had global aspirations, but the present form of globalization constitutes a profound challenge to the hegemonic ambitions of the church.

The idea that Seattle 1999 constituted a real turning point certainly cannot be fully investigated here, not least because not enough time has elapsed since then to estimate with any confidence that Seattle did, so to say, alter in a very significant way our orientations toward, to use the term yet again, globalization. The more important point is, however, that Seattle 1999 does constitute a *symbolic* representation of a major turn in the general and diffuse conceptions of globalization and globality. Suffice it to say that among many of those who might loosely be described as global activists, as opposed to relatively detached analysts, although there can be no clear distinction between the two, Seattle has become symbolic of fundamental changes with respect to the relationships between the local and the global, as well as the particular and the universal. Since Seattle the rallying cry appears to be *global* action is required to confront perceived exploiters of the deprived, the poor, the oppressed, and so on; or that "localization" can only be achieved globally (Hines 2000). And this is precisely one point where religion becomes particularly salient.

❋

Religion and Economic Globalization

Frequently but not exclusively in the relatively short history of the explicit discourse of globalization (c. 1980 onward), religion has been treated in terms of "local" religious traditions being swept by a wave of secular and homogenizing, consumerist forces. Indeed, it is common for some analysts and activists to equate globalization with the homogenization of culture and social practice (see, e.g., the truly egregious comments of Halliday 2001). In contrast, there are those who have joined me in resisting this tendency, by conceptualizing globalization as a complex mixture of homogeneity and heterogeneity—more specifically as involving the universalization of particularity and difference (as well as the particularization of universality and sameness). The latter is, I argue, an evident feature of religion in our time. So my emphasis on what I call difference-within-sameness—or, perhaps, we could say, sameness-within-difference—has both theoretical and empirical features.

It should be added that there are many in the field, broadly conceived, of religious studies who have focused on such issues as the "spiritual meaning" of globalization itself (in its most comprehensive sense), the role of ecumenicism in the globalization process, the viability of a religiously grounded global ethic, and so on. Moreover, some academic writers (e.g., Robertson 1992; Beyer 1994) have emphatically resisted limiting the focus on religion in relation to globalization to the prospects for survival of established religious traditions, large or small, old or new. Rather, they have embraced globalization as an empirical development that is the occasion for the elaboration of new ideas about religion and the world, as well as new developments in the field of religion itself.

Nonetheless, globalization has, for many speaking from within religious organizations and movements, now become something like the Antichrist, at least in areas where Christianity prevails. Parallel views are to be found in areas where other major religions are dominant, such as Muslim regions. The pope has made, as I have already emphasized, numerous pronouncements against globalization, and attacks on the inequities and injustices allegedly produced by globalization (as a primarily economic phenomenon) are very common among Catholics deeply concerned about injustice in the contemporary world as a whole. In this regard it is indeed strange that academic Catholics have seemingly ignored the intellectual debate about globalization and rushed into the arms of Catholic resistance to (allegedly) economic definitions of globalization. But such orientations toward what is in popular discourse called globalization are not by any means confined to Catholics among adherents to Christianity. They are also to be found among a number of relatively "left" Protestants. Protestants of the ideological right have, on the other hand, by and large welcomed globalization—in the narrow, fashionable sense of the shift to global capitalism, as well as the somewhat broader sense of providing more space for evangelical work, notably in ostensibly post-Communist areas in Eastern Europe and Asia, not to speak of Latin America and Africa. In spite of this, however, the ideology of "antiglobalism" and the pejorative use of terms like *one-worldism* are strong themes on the right wing of fundamental evangelicalism, notably in the United States (e.g., Bowen 1984). There has been much debate as to whether the extension of capitalism and the global expansion of evangelistic Protestantism, with more than a fundamentalist tinge, especially in Latin America, constitute a definite alliance or whether, on the other hand, the relationship between the two trends is more subtle than this.

What, then, is most significant about the Seattle turn is that antiglobalization activists and groups have in recent years become global—or, at least, transnational—actors themselves. This had become a very significant phenomenon among movements of indigenous peoples well before Seattle, but the latter was more dramatic and attracted much more attention, although indigenous movements were certainly not absent from the carnival-like events in that city. To use the word *carnival* in this context is not at all a cynical move. For there is undoubtedly a fusion of what we (older) moderns have got used to thinking about as entirely separate forms of practice. One of the most interesting things about demonstrations since 1968 has been their ritualistic-carnivalistic character, combining aspects of "orgiastic" liminality with extremely "serious" purposes, this distinction running parallel to Juergensmeyer's (2000) twofold image of religious terrorism as consisting in varying degrees of "strategic" and "symbolic" violence (123). This was certainly a feature of the World Trade Center attack in 2001, but also in a milder form in Seattle 1999, as well as of some subsequent "demofestivals." Lest, however, we forget the "more serious" side of Seattle et al., it must be remarked that antiglobal events of the recent past have brought into sharp relief a new internationalism in the labor movement.

Antiglobal movements have inexorably become part of the globalization process itself. This is so because the two primary aspects of globalization considered in its comprehensive, as opposed to its economistic, sense are rapidly increasing global connectivity, on the one hand, and fast-expanding and intensifying reflexive global consciousness, on the other. The reflexivity of contemporary global consciousness is to be witnessed precisely in the fact that ostensibly antiglobal movements represent a crucial enhancement of such reflexivity. This, I think, is something that movements previously claiming to be antiglobal now increasingly recognize. For they are becoming self-consciously global participants in a massive, although obviously contested, reflection on what is means to live in the world as a whole and the manifold ways in which questions previously thought to have only a national or regional significance now clearly have global import. This largely accounts for the not inconsiderable talk recently about "globalization from below" (e.g., Falk 1999). In other words, influential participants in what were thought of initially as antiglobal movements began to realize, with assistance from Internet culture, that to act antiglobally, one has also to act globally.

Inevitably, when we begin to consider the very closely connected circumstances in the global arena of our time in the light cast by this reflexive consciousness, spiritual issues come to the fore. For it is difficult to envisage such a form of collective consciousness as not involving what we have conventionally thought of as religious matters, quite apart from the carnivalistic and ritualistic themes I have invoked. This is most easily seen, perhaps, in controversies of an environmental nature that have been addressed by the German sociologist Ulrich Beck (1999) within the framework of "world risk society." But it is also to be seen more obliquely in the less easily specifiable enhancement of interest in matters religious, as well as theological themes, among social and cultural theorists who only a few years ago would have proclaimed themselves to be and to have heretofore been considered as secularists uninterested in religion.

It is, therefore, not easy—I would suggest not really worthwhile —attempting to separate sharply the religious from the nonreligious within the frame of the present discussion. About six weeks before the Seattle events, Barry Coates (director of the World Development Movement) wrote that the massive protests which he forecast were about to take place in the Pacific Northwest would involve "trade unions, consumer groups, farmers, indigenous peoples, antipoverty campaigners, aid agencies, academics, churches, environmentalists, animal rights activists and women's groups" (Coates 1999:29). Coates turned out to be more or less correct in his predictions, save for the attention that was, during and after the Seattle events, paid to the revival of anarchism, particularly of the northwestern United States variety. Moreover, in the actual reporting of what occurred in Seattle toward the end of 1999, little attention was, in fact, paid to "the protest's religious dimension" (Killen 2000:13).

Killen (2000) remarks on the "interfaith ecumenicism among religious traditions" in the Seattle protests and makes the interesting comment that "in the cultural quasi-anarchy of the Pacific Northwest, what made the protest possible was the fluidity of social boundaries—between rich and poor, young and old, union and non-union, religious and non-religious" (14). But in spite of Killen's not unpersuasive stress on the particularly heterogeneous culture of the Pacific Northwest, one should not overlook the claim of MacKinnon (2000) that big battles against the WTO "could happen in anytown, United States" (70) pointing to the fact that cities such as Austin, Boulder, and Indianapolis have passed "precautionary declarations" on globalization in an effort to create what has been called "an immune system against the WTO at a local level" (quoted by MacKinnon 2000). MacKinnon nonetheless both draws, inadvertently, attention to the United States as a center of antiglobality and overlooks, on the other hand, the extent to which antiglobality is itself a globalized phenomenon. The former is particularly ironic in view of the fact that the United States is frequently, as I have already remarked, identified—particularly on "the left"—as the repository and promoter of institutionalized global*ism* and the vehicle of the "new imperialism" (Biel 2000).

✳

The Crushing of "Local" Religion?

Over the past ten or more years one frequently has heard concerns raised regarding the future of local or indigenous religious traditions in the face of the sweep of globalizing tendencies. In recent years this worry has been compounded by Huntington's (1996) controversial argument about the "clash of civilizations." Yet there are several factors that counter the notion that local religions are particularly vulnerable at the present time. (1) Among these is the fact that there is a willfully nostalgic component involved in much of this argument. Moreover, in this age of the reflexive *invention or manipulation of tradition*, the prospects for many traditions—"authentic" or not—are particularly bright, not least because of their commodification in the name of the "heritage industry," in which process many representatives of traditions are certainly not unreluctant participants. It should be observed, however, that in debates to date about what are called "cultural goods" in international trade agreements, such as those in the WTO, the North American Free Trade Agreement (NAFTA), and the Organization for Economic Co-operation and Development (OECD), religion per se is not often treated as a cultural good or a component of the "culture industry" (Arizpe and Alonso 1999). In these days of "faith tourism" it seems strange that religion has not, by now, been fully regarded as a cultural good. This is *not*, however, to say that religion *should* be so identified. Nonetheless, it would appear to be inevitable that in countries, such as Turkey and Israel, that are so rich in sites of great significance in the history of Abrahamic religions, religion is rapidly becoming, or is already, a cultural commodity. This is not without irony in the case of Turkey, where successive regimes since the Turkish Republic was founded in 1923 have been militantly insistent in claiming that Turkey is a secular society. Thus ensures the ironic touristic message: come to Turkey for religious experience, even though you will be in a thoroughly secular—indeed, antireligious —society.

Space precludes much discussion of the highly problematic issue of authenticity. However, it can be mentioned here that there is an interesting parallel between what is usually called world music and the traditional cultures and religions of the world. In the quickly burgeoning, and very profitable, field of world music the paramount intellectual controversy concerns the matter as to whether local traditions are being patronized and critically evaluated in terms of their authenticity. Specifically, many local musicians have been criticized for being too international and/or commercial and insufficiently authentic. Their very global popularity is thus sometimes taken as a sign of their inauthenticity. Thus in the case of religion we find an almost globewide hybridization of indigenous religious beliefs and practices, on the one hand, and employment of modern, "Western" popular music and forms of representation and ritual, on the other. This phenomenon is particularly evident in some of the newer religious movements in Japan. .

Another parallel is provided by the native Indians—or members of First Nations—of Canada and the United States. To quote from a newspaper commentary on a recent BBC TV program: "While Indian children were forcibly sent to boarding schools and made to lose their culture, white American boys were donning Indian headdress and whooping around camp fires." The commentator, Mary Novakovich (2000), goes on to say that this contradiction includes "environmentalists' attitudes: lobbyists . . . crudely use Indians as a symbol of people at one with nature, but only if Indian ways [conform] with their own" (24).

A very different facet of this issue of local traditions is described by Juergensmeyer (1993) in his discussion of religious nationalism, when he claimed that "religious nationalists are more than just religious fanatics: they are political activists seriously attempting to reformulate the modern language of politics and provide a new basis for the nation-state" (xiii). Here again we find a disinclination to make a clear distinction between the religious and the nonreligious. But the more important point is that Juergensmeyer views "religious nationalism" as an attempt to reconstitute the *discourse* of contemporary politics. As is by now well established, control of discourse is a vital part of the so-called knowledge-power relationship, this having been a central motif in the later writings of Michel Foucault. Or, to put the issue in very different terms, religion is, as Saint-Simon observed, the primary political institution, an argument that was strongly echoed in the work of Tocqueville—and not infrequently invoked by American intellectuals and politicians, particularly those on the right wing of the ideological spectrum, as a feature of the modern United States.

So the problematic as to whether local religion is in danger from the spread of an allegedly homogenizing, mainly secular, culture (of Western origin) is exceedingly more complex than it is often made out to be. Full exploration of this issue would include much discussion of the increasingly significant but thorny question of religion and human rights, not to speak of the insecurities arising, as I have intimated, from virtually all religious traditions from ongoing processes of relativization. These processes have been responsible for the recent and widespread interest in so-called fundamentalism. As has been cogently stated, "when religion manifests itself politically in the contemporary world, it is conceptualized as *fundamentalism*" (van der Veer and Lehmann 1999:3). In other words, "fundamentalism" is, or is perceived to be, a consequence of relativization.

Certainly processes of relativization of religious beliefs and practices have been occurring throughout the history of humanity, but these have become increasingly evident as the world as a whole is being so rapidly globalized. Original Fundamentalism grew, of course, in the United States in the late nineteenth century and first quarter of the twentieth century. American Fundamentalism was in a number of respects a reaction against the perceived threat of relativization of American Protestantism by other religio-cultural doctrinal tendencies, such as German theology, Judaism and nascent Zionism, and Catholicism—not to speak of the growing challenge of European, notably Russian, socialism or communism.

The reaction against the growing Jewish presence, particularly in the state of New York, was a defensive one—that is, back to the Christian fundamentals, pivoted on the norm of Biblical inerrancy —not least because Jews began to constitute a significant electoral presence in New York and adjacent states. It is fruitful to fast-forward by about fifty years to highlight the links that began to develop in the 1970s between American Fundamentalism and Zionistic fundamentalism. While not, in a clear-cut way, an example of *anti*global religiosity, the alliance that grew between American Fundamentalists (previously though to be anti-Semitic) and Jewish Zionists is a classic, recent example of the ways in which matters religious (or, better, politico-religious) have become transnationalized and globalized.

In fact, "fundamentalism" provides some fertile ground for the exploration of antiglobal religious movements and trends. I have serious reservations about the loose use of this term, but movements usually classified as fundamentalist have certainly been primary examples of "rage against the global machine" of globalization. Micklethwait and Wooldridge (2000), in their brief but insightful comment on "the backlash against globalization" (275), consider this theme, as I have been doing, primarily in a post-Seattle perspective and, in this regard, draw attention to the Christian Identity movement in the United States, a member of which may have been involved in planting a bomb at the Olympics in Atlanta in 1996 on the grounds that the Olympic Games represent the apotheosis of race mixing and one-worldism. The line between what is and what is not religious becomes particularly evident in this connection and, in fact, illustrates the futility of striving to establish a boundary. Micklethwait and Wooldridge say that the antiglobal movement's war cry is that "every day, God-fearing Americans are being turned into slaves in a worldwide plantation economy . . . and the only way to avoid enslavement is to take up guns and fight" (275).

Beyond the United States, antiglobal movements are related to their American counterparts in the sense that they apparently feel, or exploit the feeling, that massive forces are overwhelming them. In contrast, however, they see the United States as "not the slave but the enslaver" (Micklethwait and Wooldridge 2000:275) and provide three major examples of antiglobalism: the Aum Shinrikyo movement based in Japan; the Zapatistas in Chiapas, Mexico; and what they describe as "the most powerful antiglobalist group [of] militant Islam" (276–78).

The "Militant Islam" of groups such as Osama bin Laden's al Qaeda movement is, however, a somewhat problematic example of an antiglobal movement or tendency. Indeed, Micklethwait and Wooldridge (2000) admit as much when they subsequently contend that what they call militant Islam "may be an exercise in globalization in its own right" (276). The thesis that I would propose is that Islam generally, but "militant Islam" in particular, is certainly opposed to the present form of globalization, but that far from being doctrinally and ideologically opposed to globalization per se— like much of Catholicism, evangelical Protestantism, communism, even Buddhism, not to speak of certain imperialisms (often combining religious with political and economic ambitions)—"militant Islam" has a definitely pro-global stance. In fact, one could go further than this and propose that the general orientation in Islam throughout much, if not all, of its history has been in the direction of *world encompassment*. Its tendencies in this respect are well exemplified in the history of the Ottoman Empire.

In the history of the (Muslim) Ottoman Empire extending at one stage from southeastern—indeed central—Europe round the eastern Mediterranean across North Africa into Iberia, perhaps its most central feature was its calibrated acceptance of religiocultural variety and heterogeneity. This was institutionalized as the millet system, an imperial-organizational arrangement that allowed different religio-cultural "domains" a high degree of autonomy within their respective spaces. My main point in raising this feature of the Ottoman Empire is to suggest that in a number of ways Islam, at least in its Ottoman version, provided a template as to how the world as a whole might be institutionally patterned.

As Pasha and Samatar (1997) maintain, "while elements of Westernization and capitalism are both important to globality, the notion critical [to us] is an appreciation of globality as the product of an intercivilizational encounter and dialogue" (191). They specifically address Islam, but their claim is differentially generalizable to the history of the entire world and is also very close to my own conception of what we should mean when we speak of globalization (Robertson 1992). Indeed, to conceive of globalization as being centered empirically, over a very long period of history, on intercivilizational encounters, in which religion has pivotally figured, is a particularly effective and cogent procedure.

There are several ways in which this concept of globalization relates to the seemingly antiglobal attacks by al Qaeda on September 11, 2001. First, it seems in the days immediately following 9/11 that the antiglobalization movement generally would be morally undermined by the formidable enemy of militant, anti-American Islam in the form of al Qaeda, apparently led by Osama bin Laden. However, it quickly became apparent that the antiglobalization movement—in spite of its increasing tendency to identify itself as an anticapitalist or simply an anti-American movement—had not been weakened by 9/11. In various parts of the world, including Europe, the United States was, in spite of its having been a national victim in the events of 9/11, increasingly also the target of opposition, apparently for its government's Manichean depiction of the "war" or "crusade" against terrorism; its excessive flag-waving self-pity; and its seeming McCarthy-like dichotomization of patriots versus "un-Americans" within the United States. In any case, 9/11 came during a period of increasing moral panic about the supposed cultural imperialism and politicoeconomic hegemony on the part of the United States that may well have shaped the decision to attack in September 2001.

Second, the War Against Terrorism declared by the Bush administration—strongly backed by the Blair government in the United Kingdom, and to lesser and varying degrees by some other governments—had the effect of legitimating opposition to all kinds of independence movements around the world. In this respect one of the most significant ramifications of 9/11 was to provide justification for Russian actions against Chechnya, Israeli actions against Palestinians, and various other attempts to crush so-called terrorist movements.

Third, the place of religion in all this is important but certainly not easy to identify. Undoubtedly, 9/11 was undertaken largely in the name of Islam, specifically as a theologically legitimated *jihad*. But the distinction between the religious and the political is relatively alien to much of Islamic culture, thus identifying al Qaeda and associated movements as *either* religious or political is virtually impossible. Bearing this in mind, 9/11 and its aftermath have undoubtedly put to rest the view that Islam is straightforwardly antiglobal. There were significant antiglobalization movements in predominantly Muslim countries well before 9/11. But these were apparently directed at globalization as a mainly American-directed, *economic* phenomenon. But in the more comprehensive sense of globalization—so as to include cultural, social and political, as well as economic dimensions—Islam is very much in favor of globality. Islamic globality has historically involved Islamic supremacy as an aspiration, but a supremacy that is relatively tolerant of the subsidiary existence of other religions, as was evident in the heyday of the Ottoman Empire. Bin Laden is reported to aspire, or to have aspired (if he is no longer alive), to the restoration of the Caliphate, the symbolic center of potentially worldwide Islam.

✳

Conclusion

The fact that capitalistic, economic globalization has become such a conspicuous theme of the late twentieth and early twenty-first centuries and a focus of much religious concern, indeed discontent, should not trap us into admission that this phenomenon of recent times is or has been the key feature of globalization. How we define the latter is a matter for well-informed dialogue between and among serious—as opposed to dogmatic and/or flippant—intellectuals. And yet, on the other hand, we cannot override the empirical reality of quotidian discourses and rhetorical exchanges concerning globalization.

In concluding, I should summarize the thrust of my argument.

To me, and to quite a considerable number of social scientists and scholars of religion, the concept of globalization refers in a comprehensive form—mainly cultural (including religious); political; economic; and social-communicative dimensions—to global change in recorded history (a not unproblematic phrase) that has led to our now living in what I call a "single place." In spite of this embracive conception of globalization—to which I continue, vigorously, to adhere—I have concentrated in the present deliberation mainly, but not exclusively, on the ways in which there has arisen in various parts of the world discontent with a truncated, economistic version of globalization, a discontent that has significant religious elements.

Thus there has been, in effect, a detachment of the economic from the other dimensions of globalization. And even though much of the early elaboration of the concept of globalization was undertaken by sociologists of religion and people working in the fields of religious studies, comparative religion, and theology in the late 1970s and early 1980s and was enlarged by practitioners in cultural studies, anthropology, and other disciplinary adherents, globalization is overwhelmingly now seen as a primarily economic phenomenon. But, as I have said, we cannot nor should we attempt to obliterate what has now appeared as a target of partly religious opposition—namely, globalization. The term is for some a significant theological one, whereas for others it is an evil manifestation of the antireligious, secular world in which we inevitably live.

11 ✴ *The Global Future of Religion*

NINIAN SMART

The present state of the world—one of intense globalization
—has its effect on religion. In a time when travel is almost
instantaneous, and communications wholly so, and trade is conducted everywhere, all aspects of life are affected. In addition to
the fast physical togetherness of the globalized world, there are
close ties of communication via radio, television, and now the Internet. Papua New Guinea is connected to London, Moscow to
Cape Town, Hong Kong to Santiago, Tonga to Kazakhstan. This
amazing interconnectedness has, of course, had its influence on
how people live and think.

As any acquaintance with the history of religions will show, especially in the last 400 years, faiths alter. There are evolutionary
changes in their rituals, their societal emplacement, their doctrines,
and perhaps especially their ethics and laws. One of the great myths
is that religion is always the same: that an evangelical from Mis-
souri has the same values as the apostle Paul, for example. People
dearly believe that they believe exactly as did their forefathers. They
may of course get the heart of their faith essentially right—they
may conform to the basic values of the great leaders and creeds of
their traditions. But this does not mean that the religions have not

changed. In a global world they are probably doing so more than ever.

One of the first aspects of globalization to develop in the modern era was in sea travel, which bore almost inevitably the tides of European colonialism. The Chinese, admittedly, had been great navigators, traveling as far as the African continent. But it was a series of European seamen who virtually conquered the world: Columbus, Magellan, Drake, Captain Cook. In their wake came gunboats and eventually battleships. Colonial conquest ensued. After World War II the colonies of seaborne Europe faded and were quietly extinguished. Oddly, it was the land empires that lived on: the Soviet empire survived until the closing years of the twentieth century. The Chinese one is still with us, but it will also in due course crumble. The collapse of empires resulted in roughly sovereign countries, based on linguistic and other criteria of nationhood. Yet as the colonial empires faded, so did the sovereign states.

Though the seaborne, mostly colonial, connections remain the antecedents of our global world, it is the great land-based empires that have had the most immediate impact. The Soviet Union was a reformed version of the Russian empire. After it collapsed, it fragmented into disparate states—such as Kazakhstan and Ukraine. But the Russian Federation, the USSR's residue, still remained an empire—as rebellious regions such as Chechnya discovered. The other great enduring empire is China. About half of it is the region populated by the Han Chinese, the rest by Tibet, the Uighurs, Inner Mongolia, and other areas. We have been accustomed to thinking that imperialism involved overseas adventures. It was thought that the land expansion of the Soviets was not imperialist, nor that of the Chinese. It came to many people as a bit of a shock when former president Ronald Reagan spoke of the USSR as an "evil empire." He was not, however, entirely wrong—it, like China, was an empire. But both of these empires badly needed development, and eventually the Soviet one came apart. In the Chinese sphere, eventually Tibet and the others will also become sovereign states. Empires cannot be sustained in a global world, and China will eventually break up. The inexorable demands of sovereignty by those defining themselves as a "people" will be realized (even though many aspects of nationalism are now fading through global interaction).

The great empires of the modern world needed ideologies to justify their existences. The Soviets and the Chinese employed varying forms of Marxism. The British had an ideological version of Christian civilization. But when the varied empires from Europe faded and dwindled after World War II, they retained a residue of thinking that is still with us in the global world. The non-Marxist colonial ideologies had been built on three central ideas: an expansive nationalism, democracy (at least up to a point), and capitalism. In a postcolonial era, expansive nationalism was wiped away (though a bit of superiority remained), and older ideologies resumed their places of prominence: Hindu, Muslim, and Buddhist values reentered the public sphere. The European ideal of a global Christendom retreated as various forms of Asian values permeated Christianity, African varieties of Christianity emerged in the form of new religious movements, and everywhere indigenous themes were incorporated into Christian beliefs.

This cultural interaction increased due to demographic shifts. Globalization and its preceding colonialism led to the proliferation of diasporas. The slave trade created a large African culture in South, Central, and North America. The subsequent suppression of slavery by the British navy led to a substitute: indentured labor. This labor traffic led to new outposts of Asian culture. Sizable Indian settlements were established in South Africa, East Africa, Guyana, Trinidad, Fiji, and other regions of the empire. Major subcolonies of Chinese were located in what is now called Malaysia, Indonesia, Singapore, and the Americas. Japanese migrated to the United States and South America.

Mobility has been greatly enhanced by the advent of the airplane, and during World War II the astonishing development of the jet. By 1970 jets had become jumbo jets, such as the 747. These developments meant that now everywhere was connected to everywhere. Of course on the whole it is people from richer societies who are able to travel hither and thither. But freight planes also ply the globe, so virtually every capital of the world receives goods from one another. An easy mobility has enhanced the spread of populations and the emergence of diasporic cultures around the globe.

After World War II a heavy flow of migration from India and Pakistan entered into Britain; Turks came into Germany; North Africans (notably Algerians) settled France; and later Vietnamese arrived in Australia and the United States. This demographic pattern—a northward pressure into Europe, coupled with a westward influx following the collapse of the Soviet Union, and a northward flow into the United States from Latin America—will likely increase over the years. To these population shifts one must add the migrations fomented by wars. The displacement of populations has multiplied as small but bitter conflicts have broken out in the latter part of the twentieth century in Cyprus, Indonesia, Sri Lanka, Kashmir, Afghanistan, Iraq, Iran, the Congo, West Africa, and numerous other places. Displacements have also resulted from rivalries between old neighbors: Palestinian Muslims and Israeli Jews, Orthodox Christians and Muslims in former Yugoslavia, Muslims and Christians in the Moluccas, and Christians and Hindus in Fiji.

In this global pluralism, suspicions abound. Religions have reinforced nationalism and ethnic divisions (and in some cases replaced them) as a reason for hating or suspecting "otherness." Religion is sometimes perceived as the reason for ethnic and national division, and it often gives ideological bases for the conflicts. Despite religion's ability to impart positive values about life, it can be a basis for the negative. As the pope has learned in Northern Ireland, it is not enough to say, "love they neighbor as thyself"—the admonition often falls on deaf ears. It is difficult for most religious persons to fathom how much hypocrisy and hatred are associated with religion in contentious areas of the world; it is easy to assume that religion's moral high ground will be realized.

Ideologies, whether religious or otherwise, allow people to do frightful things in their names with a feeling of justification. The inquisitors, I am sure, were not cruel men; nor were the colonializers in Britain who organized the empire; nor were the Chinese leaders who ordered troops into Tiananmen Square. It is good to remember that even some Nazis were squeamish about what they were doing and did not want to confront the consequences of their ideology. Palestinians who want Jews to be driven into the sea do not want children to be treated in that way, and perhaps they do not really want their rhetoric to be turned into ugly reality. Alas, however, firmly held convictions, though praised by many, can often lead to unimaginable cruelties.

On the positive side of global cultural encounters is the promise of dialogue. The living religions of the world usually have some elements within them—often the elites—who are willing to reach out and explore the similarities and differences among the faiths. Their aim is to provide mutual education. These gestures occur even in the midst of the most bitter divergences between peoples. In Israel, for instance, there is the *Peace Now* movement. Britain has the World Congress of Faiths. Such organizations devoted to harmony abound. And in ordinary lives of common folk in pluralistic societies often such goodwill abounds as well, though of course there is always a darker side that needs to be reckoned with.

Another positive development is mutual interaction. In addition to harmony and dialogue, religions and ideologies sometimes affect one another; there are crossovers. Liberation theology in the 1980s and 1990s, for example, provided an interesting mingling of Marxism and Catholic Christianity. In South India, Dharmaram College was the center of a strong and flourishing movement to blend Christian and Hindu thought. In parts of the Americas we find various ways of merging Catholic Christianity with African religions in mixtures such as Haitian Vodou. One of the most significant blending of ideas is that between traditional religion and Enlightenment values, leading to the modernist point of view that is found in most faiths today. The modernist strand opens up religions to scientific and scholarly ideas and practices. It opens up religions to change. It is these various forms of blending of ideas from religions and ideologies that offer hints at the possibility of a global ideology drawn from various sources—an idea to which I will soon return.

Yet at the same time that religions have been more open to one another, there has also been a significant tendency in the other direction, toward consolidation of traditional values. Ironically, the same global communication that makes possible increased interaction provides the resources for more intense consolidation as well. This is true of conservative religion, but it is also true of humanism. Humanism is an important worldview, one often neglected in discussions of religions. Yet it is the dominant faith among many modernists, especially scholars and philosophers in the West. If one adds humanism to the list of major world religions, and also adds those smaller religions that still survive in what is moving toward a global federalism of religions, the incompatibilities among worldviews are considerable. The likelihood is that in the future these differences will continue.

This is not necessarily a bad thing. Mutual criticism among

worldviews has its merits. It prevents any single worldview from dogmatism and exclusivity. The awareness of the pluralism of worldviews has the advantage of allowing each religion to adapt to the complexities of a global world. The ideology of modernism may still attempt to exert its superiority and unnerve those who otherwise would be able to feel at home in their traditions in the contemporary world. Egoism is a powerful force, but it often comes from its social milieu; and both other cultures and other faiths can threaten it.

In such a context, what possibilities exist for a common ideology for the new global world? One value that might be a part of this common ideology is the commitment to seek nonviolent solutions in situations of conflict. A remarkable aspect of our times is the way that, in part because of religious and humanistic values, great tyrannies have collapsed with scarcely any bloodshed. Consider Czechoslovakia's Velvet Revolution, and most other Eastern European rejections of the Soviets' grip; the Philippines' ouster of Marcos; Indonesia's overthrow of Suharto; Nigeria's return to democracy; South Africa's rebuke of apartheid; Peru's rejection of Fujimori; the ending of Chile's dictatorship; and the gradual democratization of Cambodia (following, however, a ghastly genocide). The peaceful aspects of these transitions are encouraging signs. They indicate an awareness that bloodshed is not the only way, and that it can have dangerous repercussions in an interconnected world. It can be countered that sometimes violence is necessary in the face of great evil—a Hitler, for example, or Stalin. Yet there are hopeful signs that the world has changed: the great totalitarian empires are dead, every dictatorship is under the bright light of global journalism, citizens everywhere have e-mail and other forms of electronic communications, and the best that any tyrannical control over information can achieve is a partial concealment. This openness is one of the great merits of globalization.

Another widely accepted value in a global world is democracy. Democracy as it is usually understood and accepted is the best nonviolent means of changing regimes. It allows people their say. It gives the majority of folks the opportunity to express their values and their grievances. It is not, however, without its defects: the majority, for example, can in the name of democracy oppress minorities. Moreover, the global world is not composed solely of sovereign states, democratic or not: it also consists of hundreds, if not thousands, of transnational corporations, some of which have larger economies and are more politically important than many sovereign states. The world also consists of great religions and their organizations: Christianity—or more correctly its three main branches, Islam in two or more forms, Judaism in its various shades, Buddhism in three major branches, Hinduism and Sikhism, Chinese values, African values, and many other traditions and groups. These three worldwide entities interact with each other— states, corporations, and worldviews. Each has exercised its powers in the recent world. Consider, for example, how the pope and the Dalai Lama have influenced the course of international affairs. Already the conference of Islamic states is being taken seriously in the world; Judaism has its political clout both through U.S. policy and the State of Israel; Hinduism is beginning to flex its muscles through political parties in the Republic of India; and in South Africa the various Christian groups have considerable influence.

This, then, is a portent of the future: two seemingly opposite trends. On the one hand, the great religious traditions—including, as I have said, humanism—are part of the global world, and because of their size and ambivalent relationship to political authority they are vital actors in it. Yet they disagree with each other over much, including the nature of ultimate reality. Some are theistic, others are not; they have divergent gods. As I have mentioned before, however, this is not necessarily a bad thing, since their very differences enable them to keep each other in check. But in order to do so, it is vital that they respect one another. They should seek to understand one another so that their divergences of ethical and other messages are kept in play.

This means that in addition to a congeries of different religions in the world it will be essential for there to be some overarching sense of order and respect. The worldview that is emerging for the global world therefore, is in essence a kind of higher order. That is, it does not lay down who is right or wrong but rather determines how peacefully the differing groups and beliefs can live together. It provides the civility, the common rules, so that one particular worldview cannot use force to establish itself over others.

Yet even if this higher order comes about, it would not necessarily guarantee the end of discord. The globe always has had and will continue to have people who for religious or other ideological reasons feel called upon to blow up citizens of other countries,

countries that they deem as oppressive. There might also be the use of weapons of mass destruction for religious purposes to destroy a New York or a Congo-Braazavile. Perhaps such an atrocity would bring the world to its senses, much as the bombs at Hiroshima and Nagasaki frightened the world so much that thus far these events have never been repeated. The hope is that even if there were such a religious disaster—the first major crime of the twenty-first century—its sheer terror would ensure that it would never be repeated. A disaster felt here is a disaster felt everywhere, in an integrated world.

All this is speculative, about a higher order that will become the global worldview. Yet the necessities of global interaction may force it upon us. The threat of globalization is that it tries to get everyone doing the same thing and thinking alike. In some ways the world is becoming too compact. The idea of a global higher order has the advantage of not imposing a single ethic or ethos on the rest of the world, except for the higher-order pattern of civility. It may be the coming global civilization.

✳ References

Abdul-Raheem, T., ed. 1966. *Pan Africanism: Politics, Economy and Social Change in the Twenty-first Century*. London: Pluto.

Alston, P. 1999. "International Governance in the Normative Areas." In *Globalization with a Human Face*, 1–36. New York: United Nations Development Programme.

Amin, S. 1997. *Capitalism in the Age of Globalization: The Management of Contemporary Society*. London: Zed Books.

Appadurai, Arjun. 1996. *Modernity at Large: Cultural Dimensions of Globalization*. Minneapolis: University of Minnesota Press.

Arizpe, L., and G. Alonso. 1999. "Culture, Globalization and International Trade." In *Globalization with a Human Face*, 37–56. New York: United Nations Development Programme.

Arjomand, S. A. 1986. "Social Change and Movements of Revitalization in Contemporary Islam." In *New Religious Movements and Rapid Social Change*, edited by James Beckford, 87–112. Thousand Oaks, Calif.: Sage.

———. 1995. "Unity and Diversity in Islamic Fundamentalism." In *Fundamentalisms Comprehended*, edited by M. Marty and R. S. Appleby, 179–98. Chicago: University of Chicago Press.

Asad, Talal. 1993. *Genealogies of Religion*. Baltimore: Johns Hopkins University Press.

Babb, Lawrence A. 1986. *Redemptive Encounters: Three Modern Styles in the Hindu Tradition*. Berkeley: University of California Press.

Barber, B. R.1995. *Jihad vs. McWorld*. New York: Random House.

Baron, Salo. 1957–83. *Social and Religious History of the Jews*. 2d ed. 18 vols. New York: Columbia University Press.

Bataille, Georges. 1988. *Inner Experience*. Translated by Leslie Ann Boldt. Albany: State University of New York Press.

Baudrillard, Jean. 1975. *The Mirror of Production*. St Louis, Mo.: Telos Press.

———. 1997. *Simulacra and Simulation*. Ann Arbor: University of Michigan Press.

Baumann, Martin. 1995. "Adapting a Religion in a Foreign Culture: Rationalist Interpretations of Buddhism in Germany." In *Buddhism and Christianity: Interactions between East and West*, edited by Ulrich Everding, 72–99. Colombo: Goethe-Institut.

Beck, U. 1999. *World Risk Society*. Cambridge: Polity Press.

Bellah, Robert. 1970. *Beyond Belief*. New York: Harper and Row.

Berger, Peter L. 1967. *The Sacred Canopy*. Garden City, N.Y.: Anchor Books.

Beyer, P. 1994. *Globalization and Religion*. London: Sage.

Biel, R. 2000. *The New Imperialism: Crisis and Contradictions in North/South Relations*. London: Zed Books.

Bowen, W. M. 1984. *Globalism: America's Demise*. Shreveport, La.: Huntington House.

Browning, D. S. 1986. "Globalization and the Task of Theological Education in North America." *Theological Education* 23(1): 43–59.

Buber, Martin. 1919. *Derheilige Weg, ein Wort an die Judenund an die Völker* (The Holy Way, a Word to the Jews and the Nations). Frankfurt am Main: Rütten & Loening.

Campbell, G. V. 1999. "The Relativization of Tradition: A Study of the Evangelical Post-Conservative Contrivers in Contemporary American Evangelical Protestantism." Ph.D. Diss. University of Pittsburgh.

Casanova, Jose. 1994. *Public Religions in the Modern World*. Chicago: University of Chicago Press.

Cesaire, Aime. 1971. *Return to My Native Land*. Paris: Presence Africaine.

Chatterji, Margaret. 1983. *Gandhi's Religious Thought*. London: Macmillan.

Clifford, James. 1997. *Routes: Travel and Translation in the Late Twentieth Century*. Cambridge, Mass.: Harvard University Press.

Coates, B. 1999. "Why Free Trade Is a Myth." *The Independent on Sunday* (UK), October 10, p. 29.

Dubnow, Simon. 1967–73. *History of the Jews*. 5 vols. Translated from the Russian, 4th definitive revised edition by Moshe Spiegel. South Brunswick, N.J.: T. Yoseloff.

Dumont, Louis. 1960. "World renunciation in Indian religions." *Contributions to Indian Sociology* 4: 33–62.

———. 1970. *Homo Hierarchicus: The Caste System and Its Implications*. Chicago: University of Chicago Press.

Durkheim, Émile. 1995 (original French, 1912). *The Elementary Forms of Religious Life*. Trans. K. Fields. New York: Free Press.

Eck, Diana. 1982. *Banaras: The City of Light*. New York: A. Knopf.

———. 2001. *A New Religious America: How a "Christian Country" Has Become the World's Most Religiously Diverse Nation*. San Francisco: Harper San Francisco.

Eickelman, D. F. 1998. "Inside the Islamic Reformation." *Wilson Quarterly* 22(1): 80–89.

Epstein, Mark. 1995. *Thoughts without a Thinker: Psychotherapy from a Buddhist Perspective*. New York: Basic Books.

Espin, Oliva. 1999. *Women Crossing Boundaries: A Psychology of Immigration and Transformations of Sexuality*. New York: Routledge.

Falk, R. 1999. *Predatory Globalization: A Critique*. Cambridge: Polity Press.

Featherstone, M., ed. 1990. *Global Culture: Nationalism, Globalization and Modernity*. London: Sage.

Finkelstein, Louis. 1924. *Jewish Self-Government in the Middle Ages*. New York: Jewish Theological Seminary of America.

Frazer, James. 1890. *The Golden Bough: A Study in Comparative Religion*. 2 vols. London: Macmillan.

———. 1918. *Folklore in the Old Testament*. 3 vols. London: Macmillan.

Freud, Sigmund. 1961. *The Future of an Illusion*. Translated by James Strachey. New York: W. W. Norton.

Frith, S. 1991. "Critical Response." In *Music at the Margins: Popular Music and Global Cultural Diversity*, edited by D. C. Robinson, E. B. Buck, and M. Cuthbert, 280–287. London: Sage.

Fronsdal, Gil. 1998. "Insight Meditation in the United States." In *The Faces of Buddhism in America*, edited by Charles S. Prebish and Kenneth K. Tanaka, 164–80. Berkeley: University of California Press.

Fuller, C. J. 1992. *The Camphor Flame: Popular Hinduism and Society in India*. Princeton, N.J.: Princeton University Press.

Gay, Peter. 1968. *The Enlightenment: An Interpretation*. New York: Viking.

Geertz, Clifford 1973. *The Interpretation of Cultures*. New York: Basic Books.

Geiger, Abraham. 1911 (original German, 1865). *Judaism and its History*. 2 pts. New York: Bloch.

Gellner, E. 1981. *Muslim Society*. Cambridge: Cambridge University Press.

Gilroy, Paul. 1993. *The Black Atlantic: Modernity and Double Consciousness*. London: Verso.

———. 1993. *Small Acts: Thoughts on the Politics of Black Cultures*. London: Serpents Tail.

Ginzberg, Louis. 1909–38. *Legends of the Jews*. 7 vols. Philadelphia: Jewish Publication Society of America.

Goitein, S. D. 1967–88. *A Mediterranean Society: The Jewish Communities of the Arab World as Portrayed in the Documents of the Cairo Geniza*. 5 vols. Berkeley: University of California Press.

Gombrich, Richard F., and Gananath Obeyesekere. 1988. *Buddhism Transformed: Recent Religious Change in Sri Lanka*. Princeton, N.J.: Princeton University Press.

Graetz, Heinrich. 1891–98 (original German, 1853–76). *History of the Jews*. 6. vols. Philadelphia: Jewish Publication Society of America.

Green, R. 1998. *A Salute to Historic African Kings and Queens*. Chicago: Empac.

Gustafson, C., and P. Juviler, eds. 1999. *Religion and Human Rights*. Armonk, N.Y.: M. E. Sharpe.

Halbfass, Wilhelm. 1990. *India and Europe: An Essay on Understanding*. Delhi: Motilal Banarsidass.

Halliday, F. 2000. *The World at 2000: Perils and Promises*. New York: Palgrave.

Hanegraaff, Wouter J. 1996. *New Age Religion and Western Culture*. Leiden: E. J. Brill.

Harris, Joseph. 1993. *Global Dimensions of the African Diaspora*. 2d ed. Washington, D.C.: Howard University Press.

Hefner, Robert. 1998. "Multiple Modernities: Christianity, Islam, and Hinduism in a Globalizing Age." *Annual Review of Anthropology* 27.

Hervieu-Leger, Daniele. 1993. "Permanence et devenir du religieux dans les societes europeenes." *Autre Temps* 38 (June): 33–34.

Hessel, Dieter T., and Rosemary Radford Reuther. 2000. *Christianity and Ecology*. Cambridge, Mass.: Harvard University Press.

Hirst, P., and G. Thompson. 1996. *Globalization in Question*. Cambridge: Polity Press.

Hobsbawm, E., and T. Ranger, eds. 1983. *The Invention of Tradition*. Cambridge: Cambridge University Press.

Hocking, William Ernest. 1940. *Living Religions and a World Faith*. New York: Macmillan.

———. 1973. *The Coming World Civilization*. Westport, Conn.: Greenwood Press.

Holton, R. J. 1998. *Globalization and the Nation-State*. New York: St. Martin's Press.

Huntington, S. 1996. *The Clash of Civilizations and the Remaking of World Order*. New York: Simon and Schuster.

Jordens, J. T. F. 1978. *Dayananda Sarasvati: His Life and Ideas*. Delhi: Oxford University Press.

Juergensmeyer, M. 1993. *The New Cold War? Religious Nationalism Confronts the Secular State*. Berkeley: University of California Press.

Juergensmeyer, M. 2000. *Terror in the Mind of God: The Global Rise of Religious Violence*. Berkeley: University of California Press.

Jules-Rosette, Bennetta. 1989. "The Sacred in African New Religions." In

The Changing Face of Religion, edited by James Beckford and Thomas Luckman. London: Sage.

Kakar, Sudhir. 1991. *The Analyst and the Mystic: Psychoanalytic Reflections on Religion and Mysticism*. Chicago: University of Chicago Press.

Kantowsky, Detlef. 1995. "Buddhist Modernism." In *Buddhism and Christianity: Interactions between East and West*, edited by Ulrich Everding, 101–15. Colombo: Goethe-Institut.

Katz, Jacob. 1961 (original Hebrew, 1958). *Tradition and Crisis*.New York: Free Press.

Kearney, M. 1995. "The Local and the Global: The Anthropology of Globalization and Transnationalism." *Annual Review of Anthropology* 24.

Killen, P. O'C. 2000."Faithless in Seattle? The WTO Protests." *Religion in the News* 3(1): 12.–14.

Klein, N. 2000. *No Logo*. London: Flamingo.

Kopf, David. 1979. *The Brahmo Samaj and the Shaping of the Modern Indian Mind*. Princeton, N.J.: Princeton University Press.

Kripal, Jeffrey J. 1995. *Kali's Child: The Mystical and the Erotic in the Life and Teachings of Ramakrishna*. Chicago: University of Chicago Press.

Lash, S., and J. Urry. 1987. *The End of Organized Capitalism*. Cambridge: Polity Press.

Lauterbach, Jacob Z. 1970. *Studies in Jewish Law, Custom, and Folklore*. Ed. B. J. Bamberger. New York: Ktav.

Lawrence, B. B. 1998. "From Fundamentalism to Fundamentalisms: A Religious Ideology in Multiple Forms." In *Religion, Modernity and Postmodernity*, edited by P. Heelas, 88–101. Oxford: Blackwell.

Luckmann, Thomas. 1967. *The Invisible Religion*. New York: Macmillan.

MacKinnon, J. 2000. "When the Global Goes Loco: The Next Big Battle Against the WTO Could Happen in Anytown, USA." *Adbusters* (June/July), pp. 70–71.

Madan, T. N. 1987. *Non-Renunciation: Themes and Interpretations of Hindu Culture*. Delhi: Oxford University Press.

———. 1998. *Modern Myths, Locked Minds: Secularism and Fundamentalism in India*. Delhi: Oxford University Press.

Madan, T. N. et al. 1971. Review Symposium on Louis Dumont's *Homo Hierarchicus*. *Contributions to Indian Sociology* 5: 1–81.

Majur, J. 2000. "Labor's New Internationalism." *Foreign Affairs* 79(1): 79–93.

Marsden, G. M. 1980. *Fundamentalism and American Culture*. New York: Oxford University Press.

Martin, David. 1978. *A General Theory of Secularization*. New York: Harper and Row.

Micklethwait, J., and A. Wooldridge. 2000. *A Future Perfect: The Challenge and Hidden Promise of Globalization*. London: William Heinemann.

Molino, Antony. 1998. *The Couch and the Tree: Dialogues in Psychoanalysis and Buddhism*. New York: North Point Press.

Nairn, T. 1988. *The Enchanted Glass: Britain and its Monarchy*. London: Hutchinson Radius.

Nandy, Ashish, Shikha Trivedy, Shail Mayaram, and Achyot Yagnik. 1995. *Creating a Nationality: The Ramjanambhumi Movement and the Fear of Self*. Delhi: Oxford University Press.

Niebuhr, Reinhold. 1959. *The Structure of Nations and Empires*. New York: Scribner.

Nietzsche, Friedrich. 1978. *Thus Spoke Zarathustra*. Translated by Walter Kaufmann. New York: Penguin.

———. 1990. *Twilight of the Idols/The Anti-Christ*. Translated by R.D. Hollingdale. London: Penguin Classics.

———. 2000. *The Birth of Tragedy*. Translated by Douglas Smith. Oxford: World Classics, 2000.

Northrop, F. S. C. 1979. *The Meeting of East and West*. Woodbridge, Conn.: Ox Bow Press.

Nossig, Alfred. 1894. *Die Sozialhygiene der Juden und des altorientischen Völkerkreis*. Stuttgart: Deutsche Verlags-Anstalt.

Novakovich, M. 2000. "Today's TV." *The Guardian*, G2 (UK), September 14, p. 24.

Nussbaum, M. C. 1996. "Patriotism and Cosmopolitanism." In *For Love of Country: Debating the Limits of Patriotism*, edited by J. Cohen. Boston: Beacon Press.

Obeyesekere, Gananath. 1972. "Religious Symbolism and Political Change in Ceylon." In *The Two Wheels of Dhamma*, edited by Bardwell L. Smith, 58–78. Chambersburg, Pa.: Wilson Books.

———. 1976. "Personal Identity and Cultural Crisis: The Case of Anagarika Dharmapala of Sri Lanka." In *The Biographical Process*, edited by Frank Reynolds and Donald Capps, 221–52. The Hague: Mouton, 1976.

———. 1991. "Buddhism and Conscience: An Exploratory Essay." *Daedalus* 120(3): 219–39.

———. 1995. "Buddhism, Nationalism and Cultural Identity." In *Fundamentalisms Comprehended*, edited by Martin E. Marty and R. Scott Appelby, 231–56. Chicago: University of Chicago Press.

———. 1995. "The Two Faces of Colonel Olcott: Buddhism and Euro-rationality in the late Nineteenth Century." In *Buddhism and Christianity: Interactions between East and West*, edited by Ulrich Everding, 32–71. Colombo: Goethe-Institut.

———. 1996. "Buddhist Identity in Sri Lanka." In, *Ethnic Identity, Creation, Conflict, and Accommodation*, 3d ed., edited by Lola Romanucci-Ross and George deVos, 222–47. Walnut Creek, Calif.: Altamira Press.

Olupona, Jacob. 2002. *African Immigrant Religious Communities: Identity Formation in America's Pluralistic Society*. The Ford Foundation.

Parsons, Talcott. 1963. "Christianity and Modern Industrial Society." In *Sociological Theory, Values and Sociocultural Change*, edited by E. A. Tiryakian, 33–70. New York: Free Press.

Pasha, M. K., and A.I. Samatar. 1997. "The Resurgence of Islam." In *Globalization: Critical Reflections*, edited by J. H. Mittelman, 187–201. Boulder, Colo.: Rienner.

Pereira de Queiroz, Isaura 1989. "Afro-Brazilian Cults and Religious Change in Brazil." In *The Changing Face of Religion*, edited by James Beckford and Thomas Luckmann, 88. London: Sage.

Popper, Karl. 1961. *The Poverty of Historicism*. London: Routledge and Kegan Paul.

Prebish, Charles S. 1979. *American Buddhism*. North Scituate, Mass.: Duxbury Press.

Proturo, Stephen. 1966. *The White Buddhist: The Asian Odyssey of Henry Steel Olcott*. Bloomington: Indiana University Press.

Redkey, E. S. 1969. *Black Exodus: Black Nationalism and Back to Africa Movements*. New Haven: Yale University Press.

Riesebrodt, Martin. 1993. *Pious Passion. The Emergence of Modern Fundamentalism in the United States and Iran*. Translated by Don Reneau. Berkeley: University of California Press.

Riesebrodt, Martin, and Mary Ellen Konieczny. Forthcoming. "Sociology of Religion." In *Penguin Companion to the Study of Religion*, edited by John Hinnells.

Robertson, R. 1985. "The Development and Implications of the Classical Sociological Perspective on Religion and Revolution." In *Religion, Rebellion, Revolution*, edited by B. Lincoln, 236–65. London: Macmillan.

———. 1988. "Christian Zionism and Jewish Zionism: Points of Contact." In *The Politics of Religion and Social Change*, edited by A. Shupe and J. K. Hadden. New York: Paragon House.

———. 1989. "Globalization, Politics, and Religion." In *The Changing Face of Religion*, edited by J.A. Beckford and T. Luckmann, 10–23. London: Sage.

———. 1992. *Globalization: Social Theory and Global Culture*. London: Sage.

———. 1994. "Religion and the Global Field." *Social Compass* 41(1): 121–135.

———. 1995. "Glocalization: Time-Space and Homogeneity-Heterogeneity." In *Global Modernities*, edited by M. Featherstone, S. Lash, and R. Robertson, 25–44. London: Sage.

———. 1995. "The Search for Fundamentals in Global Perspective." In *The Search for Fundamentals and Modernization*, edited by L. van

V. Tijsson, J. Berting, and F. Lechner, 213–231. Berlin: W. de Gruyter.

———. 2000. "Globalization and the Future of 'Traditional Religion.'" In *God and Globalization: Theological Ethics and the Spheres of Life*, vol. 1, edited by M.L Stackhouse with P.J. Paris, 53–68. Harrisburg, Pa.: Trinity Press International.

———. 2000. "Globalization Theory 2000+: Major Problematics." In *Handbook of Social Theory*, edited by G. Ritzer and B. Smart, 458–470. London: Sage.

———. 2001. "Opposition and Resistance to Globalization." In *Globalization and the Margins*, edited by J. R. Short and R. Grant. London: Palgrave.

Robertson, R., and H. H. Khondker. 1998. "Discourses of Globalization: Preliminary Considerations." *International Sociology* 13(1): 5–40.

Robertson, R., and R. Mouly. 1982. "Zionism in American Premillenarian Fundamentalism." *American Journal of Theology and Philosophy* 4(3): 97–109.

Rouner, Leroy, ed. 1966. *Philosophy, Religion, and the Coming World Civilization: Essays in Honor of William Ernest Hocking*. The Hague: Martinus Nijhoff.

Ruppin, Arthur. 1931. *Soziologie der Juden* (Sociology of the Jews). Berlin: JuedischeVerlag.

Sassen, Saskia. 1998. *Globalization and Its Discontents*. New York: New Press.

Scholem, Gershom. 1946. *Major Trends in Jewish Mysticism*. Rev. ed. New York: Schocken.

Scholte, J. A. 2000. *Globalization: A Critical Introduction*. London: Macmillan.

Sears, Laurie. 1996. *Shadows of Empire: Colonial Discourse and Javanese Tales*. Durham, N.C.: Duke University Press.

Segal, R. 1995. *The Black Diaspora*. London: Faber and Faber.

Seneviratne, H. L. 1999. *The Work of Kings: The New Buddhism of Sri Lanka*. Chicago: University of Chicago Press.

Sklair, L. 2000. *The Transnational Capitalist Class*. Oxford: Blackwell.

Smith, Wilfred Cantwell. 1991. *The Meaning and End of Religion*. Minneapolis, Minn.: Fortress Press.

Smith, William Robertson. 1894. *Lectures on the Religion of the Semites*. Revised edition. First series, The Fundamental Institutions. London: A. & C. Black.

Smith, Jonathan Z. 1982. *Imagining Religion*. Chicago: University of Chicago Press.

Spengler, Oswald. 1926. *Decline of the West*. New York: A. A. Knopf.

Spiro, Melford E. 1994. *Culture and Human Nature*. New Brunswick, N.J.: Transaction.

Srinivas, M. N. 1959. "The Dominant Caste in Rampura." *American Anthropologist* 61: 1–16.

———. 1962. *Caste in Modern India and Other Essays*. Bombay: Asia Publishing House.

Stackhouse, M. L. with P. J. Paris, eds. 2000. *God and Globalization: Theological Ethics and the Spheres of Life*. Vol. 1. Harrisburg, Pa.: Trinity Press International.

Tomlinson, J. 1999. *Globalization and Culture*. Chicago: University of Chicago Press.

Toynbee, Arnold. 1934–61. *A Study of History*. Oxford: Oxford University Press.

van der Veer, P., and H. Lehmann. 1999. "Introduction." In *Nation and Religion: Perspectives on Europe and Asia*, 3–14. Princeton, N.J.: Princeton University Press.

Verhoeven, Martin J. 1998. "Carus and the Transformation of Asian Thought." In *The Faces of Buddhism in America*, edited by Charles S. Prebish and Kenneth K Tanaka, 207–27. Berkeley: University of California Press.

Von Glasenapp, Helmuth. 1970. *Buddhism: A Non-Theistic Religion*. Trans. Irmgard Schloegl. New York: G. Braziller.

Walls, Andrew. 2000. "The Expansion of Christianity: An Interview with Andrew Walls." *Christian Century*, August 2–9, p. 795.

Warner, Stephen and Judith Witter, eds. 1998. *Gathering in Diaspora: Religious Communities and the New Immigration*. Philadelphia: Temple University Press.

Watson, J., ed. 1997. *Golden Arches East: McDonald's in East Asia*. Stanford, Calif.: Stanford University Press.

Weber, Max. 1952 (original German, 1920). *Ancient Judaism*. Translated and edited by Hans H. Gerth and Don Martindale. Glencoe, Ill.: Free Press.

———. 1949. *The Methodology of the Social Sciences*. Translated and edited by Edward A. Shils and Henry A. Finch. New York: Free Press.

———. 1958. *The Religion of India: The Sociology of Hinduism and Buddhism*. Translated and edited by Hans H. Gerth and Don Martindale. Glencoe, Ill.: Free Press, 1958.

———. 1993. *Sociology of Religion*. Trans. T. Parsons. Boston: Beacon Press.

Williams, Duncan Ryuken, and Christopher S. Queen, eds. 1999. *American Buddhism: Methods and Findings in Recent Scholarship*. Richmond, Surrey: Curzon.

Yerushalmi, Yosef, H. 1982. *Zakhor, Jewish History and Jewish Memory*. Seattle: University of Washington Press.

Yong, Amos. 1999. " 'Not Knowing Where the Wind Blows': On Envisioning a Pentecostal-Charismatic Theology of Religions." *Journal of Pentecostal Studies* 14 (April): 81–91.

Young, Lawrence A., ed. 1997. *Rational Choice Theory and Religion.* New York: Routledge.

Zunz, Leopold. 1823. "Grundlinien zueiner künftigen Statistik der Juden." *Zeitschrift für die Wissenschaft des Judentums:* 523–532.

❈ Index

ashrama, 56
Asia. *See specific countries and regions*
askesis, 77
Asoka, king of India, 63
Assyria, 45, 46
Atlanta, Ga., 84
    Olympics bombing (1996), 119–20
Augustine, Saint, 76
Aum Shinrikyo movement, 120
Australia, 87, 127
authenticity, 76, 117
Axial Age religions, 64
Ayodhya violence (India), 61–62

Babylonia. *See* Iraq
Babylonian captivity, 5, 46
Babylonian Talmud, 44, 46, 48
Bali, 4, 53
Bantu language, 84
Baptist Church, 83
Barber, B. R., 37
Baron, Salo, 41
Barth, Karl, 18, 19
Bataille, Georges, 76
Baudrillard, Jean, 70
Baumann, Martin, 69
Beck, Ulrich, 115
beef taboo (Hindu), 55
beliefs, religious, practices vs., 99–102
Bengal, 58, 60
Benin, 84
Berger, Peter, 12, 102
Bhagavad Gita, 55, 59, 71
bhakti, 59
Bharatiya Janata Party (BJP), 61, 62
Biarritz (2000) protests, 111
Bible, 4, 5, 55, 119
    Jewish canonization of, 46, 48
    New Testament, 47, 59
    sociological/anthropological ap-
        proaches to, 41–44
Bio Bio project, 91
Birth of Tragedy, The (Nietzsche), 76
Blavatsky, H. P., 67, 68–70, 71, 72
bodhi tree, 63, 66
Bonhoeffer, Dietrich, 23–24
Borabadur, 4
border crossings, 88–89

Boyarin, Daniel, 26
Brahmans, 5, 53, 54, 55, 56, 58, 59
Brahmo Samaj (society of God), 58
Brazil, 17, 84–85
British Broadcasting Corporation, 36–37,
    118
Brown, Peter, 5
Buber, Martin, 42
Buddha, 7, 54, 63, 66, 71, 72, 77
Buddhāgama, 64
Buddhism, 5, 8, 63–77, 103
    antiglobalism and, 120
    European text scholars, 65–67, 69
    geographic roots of, 3, 4, 7, 64
    globalization of, 64, 70–74
    Hinduism and, 26, 53, 68
    meditation and, 72, 73–77
    Theosophy and, 67–70
    Western, 4, 69, 71–75
    as Western neologism, 64
Buddhist Catechism, The, 68
Buddhist Theosophical Society, 68, 71

Cairo *geniza*, 44
caliphate, 29, 48, 122
Campbell, Joseph, 11–12
Canada, 3, 118
Candomble, 85
capitalism, 25, 42, 71–72, 107–8, 126
    demonstrations against, 111
    global, 65, 70, 75, 114, 121, 122
Caro, Joseph, 49
caste system, 52–53, 55, 56–57, 59, 60
catastrophe, global, 24–25, 107
Catholicism. *See* Roman Catholicism
Celestial Church of Christ (West Africa),
    81
Center for the Study of World Religions,
    Harvard University, 20
central Asia, 63, 87
Centre for the Study of Christianity in
    the Non-Western World, University
    of Edinburgh, 17
charismatic churches, 18, 82–83
Chechnya, 122, 125
Cherubim and Seraphim (West Africa),
    81
Chiapas, 26, 120

Gao, 83
Gay, Peter, 69
Geertz, Clifford, 71, 101
Geiger, Abraham, 41
Gellner, Ernest, 33
Genesis, Book of, 4
Genoa protests (2001), 111–12
Germany, 6, 69, 126
  Judaism and, 41, 48–50
Ghana, 84
Gilgamesh (Sumerian epic), 4
Ginzberg, Louis, 42
global communication. *See* communication, global
globalization
  colonial antecedents of, 125
  common ideology and, 129–30
  contemporary vs. older missionizing process, 29, 65
  cultural aspects of, 12, 113, 122, 123, 127–28
  development of, 125–27
  diasporic results of, 126–27
  economic, 25, 72, 112–16, 121, 122
  fundamentalism as reaction to, 29, 108, 114, 119–20, 122
  indigenous cultures and, 87–88, 116–22
  as intercivilizational encounters, 121, 122
  Islam and, 36–39, 122
  role of religion in, 12–13, 95–109, 121, 127
  technology and, 24, 107
  See also antiglobalization movement; *specific religions*
gnosticism, 9
God, 65, 66, 71
gods and goddesses, 5, 54–55, 60
Goenka meditation, 74
Goitein, S. D., 43, 44
Goldberg, Harvey E., 40–51
Golden Bough, The (Frazer), 42
Graetz, Heinrich, 41
Great Britain. *See* United Kingdom
great flood, 4
Greek language, 7
guru cults, 10, 60–61, 69
Guyana, 126

Haiti, 4, 85, 128
Hajj, 36
Halbfass, Wilhelm, 65
Halliday, F., 113
Hanbalism, 31, 32
Handbook of Global Religions, A, 13
Harvard University, 20, 91
haskala, 50
heaven, 9
Hebrew language, 7, 46
Hebrew University (Jerusalem), 42
Hegel, Georg Wilhelm Friedrich, 65
Heidegger, Martin, 76
Hellenism, Judaism and, 46–47
heritage industry, 117
Hibbert Lectures, 20
Hinduism, 3, 5, 52–62, 130
  anti-Muslim violence and, 61–62
  Buddhism and, 26, 53, 68
  contemporary trends in, 60–62, 72
  contrasted with other religions, 54
  definitions of, 52
  globalization of, 6, 52–53, 126
  guru cults, 10, 60–61, 69
  postcolonial era and, 126
  Theosophy and, 67, 68, 69
  as Western neologism, 53–54, 64
Hocking, William Ernest, 11, 20–21, 23, 26
Holocaust, 43, 51
Holy Spirit, 82
holy wars, 21
Homo Hierarchicus (Dumont), 56–57
humanism, 128, 130
human rights, 39, 118
Huntington, Samuel, 12, 21, 24, 116

Ifa, 85
Igbo, 83
Ile-Ife, 84, 85
imam veneration, 31
Imilgei, Sara, 90–91
immigrants. *See* diaspora
imperialism, 120, 121, 125. *See also* colonialism
indentured labor, 53, 126
independence movements, 122

India
  Buddhism in, 63, 64
  Hinduism in, 3, 5, 52–62, 130
  Hindu-Muslim violence in, 61–62
  Islam in, 3, 53
  migrants from, 126
  Theosophy and, 68
Indian National Congress, 58
indigenous cultures, 10, 87–92
  African religion and, 78, 81, 84–85, 126
  Christianity and, 5, 26, 126, 128
  commodification of, 117–18
  globalization seen as threat to, 116–22
  UN year of (1993), 91
  worldwide revival of religions, 91–92
Indonesia, 3–4, 53, 126, 129
institutionalized religion. *See* religion
International Monetary Fund, 110
International Society for Krishna Con-
    sciousness (ISKCON), 60
Internet, 74, 115, 124
interventive practices, 100–102
Inuits, 90
Iran, 8, 32, 33
  Islamic revolution (1979), 35, 36–37
Iraq (formerly Babylonia)
  Judaism and, 5, 41, 43, 44, 46, 48
  Wahhabi fundamentalists and, 32
Islam, 3, 4, 7, 8–9, 20, 25, 28–39, 130
  Africanized, 32, 33, 78, 83–84
  contemporary ideologies, 35–36
  contemporary revival of, 32–34
  defensive counter-universalism,
    38–39
  fundamentalism, 28, 31, 32, 34, 35–38
  geographic roots of, 7
  globalization of, 29–32, 33, 35, 36–38,
    64–65, 84, 120–21, 122
  Hinduism and, 53, 57, 58, 59, 61–62
  inception as global religion, 28
  Judaism and, 43, 44, 48, 49, 51
  mainstream vs. Hanbalism, 31, 32
  militant, 120–22
  orthodox reformism, 32
  political, 8–9, 34–39, 120–22
  postcolonial era and, 126
  Western cultural challenge to, 32

Islamic law, 30, 31
Israel, ancient, 5–6, 41, 42
  unity and diversity in, 44–47
Israel, State of, 40, 43, 51, 117, 130
  American Fundamentalist/Zionistic
    fundamentalist alliance and, 119
  Palestinian conflict and, 122, 128
Isserles, Moshe, 49

Jainism, 58
Jama'at-i Islami, 35
Jammu, 53
Janavasabha Sutta (Buddhist text), 66
Japan, 3, 4, 10, 118, 120
Jaspers, Karl, 64
jātakas, 66
Javanese shadow theater, 71
Jerusalem, 7, 45, 47
Jerusalem Temple
  fall of (70 C.E.), 5, 47
  fall of (586 B.C.E.), 45
  Maccabean revolt (167 B.C.E.), 47
  Second Temple period, 46
Jesus Christ, 9, 23, 58, 71
jet air travel, 127
Jewish Self-Government in the Middle Ages
    (Finkelstein), 44
Jews. *See* Judaism
jihad, 37
Josephus, 47
Joshua, 46
Jubilee 2000 (organization), 111
Judaism, 4, 40–51, 119, 130
  acculturation/transformation of, 7
  American Fundamentalism and, 119
  ancient, 4–5, 41, 42, 44–47
  Christianity's roots in, 9, 26, 42, 47
  collective memory studies, 43
  diasporic, 5–6, 40, 41, 47, 48–51
  global diversity of, 40–41, 48–49
  law, 30, 44, 48, 49
  political emancipation and, 41, 43, 50
Judea, 45–47
Judge, William Q., 67
Juergensmeyer, Mark, 3–16, 114, 118
Jung, Carl, 12
just price, 25

Orisha tradition, 85
Orthodox Judaism, 51
Oshun, 85
Ottoman Empire, 49, 120–21, 122
Oyo, 84, 85
Oyotungi Village (S.C.), 85

Pakistan, 3, 35, 38, 126
Palestine, 42, 43
Palestine Office of the Zionist Organization, 42
Palestinians, 122, 128
Palestinian Talmud, 44, 48
Pali language, 7
Pali Text Society, 66
pan-African movement, 79, 85
Panchamama (Mother Earth), 91, 92
pan-Indian identity, 54, 55
pan-Islam, 35
Pasha, M. K., 121
Passover, 47
Path of Purification (Buddhagosa), 77
patriarchal system, 107, 108
Paul, apostle, 9, 124
Peace Now movement, 128
Pentateuch, 45, 48
Pentecostalism, 18, 82–83
Pentikäinen, Juha, 87–92
Peres, Shimon, 91
Persian Empire, 29, 46
Peru, 91–92, 129
Pharisees, 42–43, 47
pilgrimage, 7, 33, 36, 61, 64
political systems
    ancient Israelites and, 45–46, 47
    democratization effects, 107
    discourse control of, 118
    fundamentalist religion and, 114,
        118–22
    global religious resurgence and, 107
    Hinduism and, 59, 61–62
    Islam and, 33, 34–36, 38–39
    Judaism and, 41, 43, 50–51
    religious nationalism and, 118
    transnational religions and, 8–9
polygamy, 49
polytheism, 32, 82
Popper, Karl, 70

postcolonial era, 126
postmodernism, 70
poststructuralism, 76
Poussin, La Valee, 66
Prabhupada, Shrila, 60
practices, religious, 99–102
Prague (2000) demonstrations, 110
prestructuralism, 89
priesthood, 45, 47, 57
Prophetic Traditions (Islam), 30, 31, 32
Prophetic writings (Judaism), 46
Protestant Buddhism, 69, 71–72
Protestant ethic, 42, 96
Protestantism, 3, 19, 42
    African mission churches and, 82–83
    economic globalization and, 114
    fundamentalism and, 119, 120
protests. *See* demonstrations
Punjab, 6–7, 58
Puranas, 51, 54, 55, 57, 60
"Puritan spirit," 96

al Qaeda, 8–9, 120, 121
Qur'an, 29–30, 31, 32, 33, 36, 54, 55
Qutb, Sayyid, 36

rabbinic Judaism, 30, 42–43, 44, 47–51
    literature of, 48, 49
Rajneesh, Acharya, 60
Ralco River, 90–91
Rama (god), 62
Ramakrishna, 58, 72
Ramayana (Hindu epic), 61
rational choice theory, 96
rationality, 65, 68, 69, 71, 75–77
    Hanbalism vs., 31
Reagan, Ronald, 125
Redfield, Robert, 88, 89
Reform Judaism, 50–51
reincarnation, 22, 56, 70
relativization, religious, 118–19
religion
    antiglobalism and, 110–23
    crises as seedbed of, 105–6
    in diaspora, 5–7
    economic globalization and, 112–16
    evolutionary changes in, 124–25
    faith tourism and, 117

Taoism, 4
Tathagata, 71
technology, 24, 107
Temple in Jerusalem. *See* Jerusalem
    Temple
temples, Buddhist, 53
terrorism, 12–13, 110, 114, 119–20, 121–22
theocracy, 35
theodicy, 56
Theosophical Society, 67, 68, 70–71
Theosophy, 67–70
Theravada Buddhism, 64, 66, 67, 68, 73, 74
Theresa, Mother, 10
Third World debt forgiveness, 111–12
Thomas, E. J., 66
Tibetan Buddhism, 3, 4, 6, 73, 74–75
Tillich, Paul, 11, 20
Timbuktu, 83
TM, 60
Tocqueville, Alexis de, 118
Toledo, Alejandro, 91–92
Torah, 46, 47, 48
totalitarianism, 35–36, 129
tourism, faith, 117
Toynbee, Arnold, 12, 19, 21, 23
trade, 83, 84, 117
traditional cultures. *See* indigenous
    cultures
Tradition and Crisis (Katz), 43
Tradition of the Prophet (Islam), 30, 31,
    32
traditions
    contemporary fundamentalist changes
        in, 108
    diasporic changes in, 7
    invention/manipulation of, 117–18
transcendental meditation, 60
transcendental philosophy, 69
transmigration of souls, 56
transnational corporations, 130
Trinidad, 6, 53, 85, 126
Troeltsch, Ernest, 78
Turkey, 117. *See also* Ottoman Empire
Tutu, Desmond, 10, 80

ulema, 30, 33
uncertainty, 106, 107
UNESCO, 89–90

United Kingdom, 121
    Asian Buddhist immigrants in, 73, 126
    colonial empire, 53, 126
    Hinduism and, 53
    Islam and, 37–38
United Nations, 38, 91
United States
    African immigrants in, 83, 85
    antiglobality and, 111, 115–16, 119–20,
        121
    Buddhism and, 4, 72, 74, 127
    Christianity and, 3, 17
    fundamentalist evangelicals and, 114,
        119
    Hinduism and, 53, 60
    indigenous peoples and, 118
    Islam and, 6
    Judaism and, 50–51
    multinational/religious pluralism of,
        4, 96
    terrorist attack on, 120–22
    Theosophy and, 67
University of Edinburgh, 17
Untouchables. *See* Scheduled Castes
urbanization
    indigenous religions and, 87
    Islamic revival and, 33, 34, 35, 37–38, 84

Vaishno Devi (goddess), 60
Vaishyas, 55
Vajrayana, 68, 74
van Gennep, Arnold, 88–89
varna, 55, 56
Vatican, 112, 113–14, 130
Vedanta, 58, 59, 65, 69, 71
Vedas, 54, 55, 57, 58, 59
Vedic tradition, 53, 54, 58, 60, 68
videos, 74
Vietnamese immigrants, 126–27
violence, religious, 36, 131
    Hindu-Muslim, 61–62
    militant Islam and, 120, 121–22
    against modernity, 12–13
    strategic and symbolic, 114
    See also terrorism
vipassana meditation, 73, 74
Vishnu (god), 55
Vishwa Hindu Parishad (VHP), 62, 63